INCLUSION VOICES

Canadian Child Care Directors
Talk About Including
Children with Special Needs

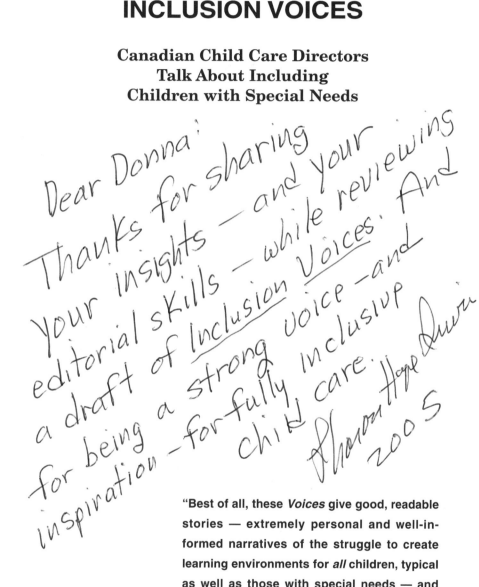

Dear Donna:
Thanks for sharing
your insights — and your
editorial skills — while reviewing
a draft of Inclusion Voices. And
for being a strong voice — and
inspiration — for fully inclusive
child care.

Sharon Hope Irwin
2005

"Best of all, these *Voices* give good, readable stories — extremely personal and well-informed narratives of the struggle to create learning environments for *all* children, typical as well as those with special needs — and keeping those settings alive."

INCLUSION VOICES

Canadian Child Care Directors Talk About Including Children with Special Needs

Sharon Hope Irwin

With an Afterward by Donna S. Lero

Breton Books

Research for *Inclusion Voices* was funded by Social Development Partnerships Program, Social Development Canada. The opinions and interpretations in this publication are those ot the author and interviewees, and do not necessarily represent those of the Government of Canada.

Editor: Ronald Caplan

Production Assistance: Bonnie Thompson, Tyana Panthier,
and Fader Communications

Cover Photographs: Katheryn Gordon

Canada Council   Conseil des Arts
for the Arts   du Canada
We acknowledge the support of the
Canada Council for the Arts for our publishing program.

We also acknowledge support from Cultural Affairs, NOVA SCOTIA
Nova Scotia Department of Tourism and Culture.   Tourism and Culture

We acknowledge the financial support of the Government of Canada
through the Book Publishing Industry Development Program (BPIDP)
for our publishing activities.   Canadä

Library and Archives Canada Cataloguing in Publication

Irwin, Sharon Hope
    Inclusion voices : Canadian child care directors talk
about including children with special needs / Sharon Hope Irwin.

ISBN 1-895415-63-2   Printed in Canada

    1. Child care–Canada. 2. Children with disabilities–
Care–Canada. 3. Children with disabilities–Services for–
Canada. 4. Child care services–Canada. I. Title.

HQ778.7.C3I778 2004   362.71'2'0870971   C2004-907198-X

CONTENTS

Acknowledgements

For their sponsorship and their belief in the importance of research on inclusive child care, our thanks to our primary sponsor, Social Development Partnerships Program, Social Development Canada, and to our project officers, Penny Hammell and Kelly King.

Our thanks to the ten centre directors who welcomed us and shared frankly both their hopes and their concerns. This book is theirs.

Our thanks to the Town Daycare Centre and Allkids Early Intervention in Glace Bay, Nova Scotia, and to the families of the children in the cover photographs.

Our thanks to the observation team — Dixie Mitchell, Leona Howard and Sherri Woitte — who braved winter storms and battled airline delays and uncleared roads in order to visit the centres.

For help in turning the transcripts into a book, our thanks to Tyana Panthier — lawyer, English literature graduate and very new mom — who has become thoroughly engaged with child care issues in her own life. Our thanks also to Catherine Stewart, Carolyn Webber, and Donna Michal for their critical readings of the text. Any errors or omissions are, of course, the responsibility of the author.

Finally, our thanks to Glenda Watt, splendid typist, and our editors, Bonnie Thompson and Ronald Caplan, for their skillful partnership in creating *Inclusion Voices*.

What the Voices Told Me

Sharon Hope Irwin

I started this search of Canadian child care centres in the hope of finding success — seeking evidence that inclusion of children with special needs was happening and working and even growing in child care centres across Canada.

I felt prepared for the job. Before making the initial visits, I had just completed fifteen years as director of a child care centre that was considered a model of inclusion in Canada. I had served as an advocate to government at all levels. Like the directors I was visiting, I knew what it was like to fight for inclusion and to try to make it a reality despite the lack of resources, training and community understanding. I had lived many of the challenges other inclusion directors face.

Now, ten years after those first visits, I returned to those same child care centres — centres that had been identified by child care organizations, disability organizations and government officials as some of the best inclusive centres across Canada. And my question was: What has happened in the past decade?

In the face of enormous fiscal restraints and cutbacks since my last visits, I wanted to know: What has happened to the kids? What has happened to the staff? What has happened to the commitment of the directors and their boards? What has happened to the level of inclusion quality in these centres? In short, What do these Inclusion Voices — the directors I met with — tell us today about Canada's future in inclusive child care?

I knew that during the past ten years child care had experienced increasing levels of staff turnover and declining enrollments in training programs. I knew that some provinces had made severe changes in their methods of supporting centres that include children with special needs. I knew that the social capital was wearing down — that the pioneers were aging and retiring or moving on. The physical capital was in peril as well: the buildings no longer met current standards. And I knew that grants and contributions for innovation were drying up, and that enthusiastic volunteers and board members were harder to find.

Still, I hoped that despite these additional difficulties, the energetic committed inclusion leaders whom I had visited ten years earlier would still be leading highly effective inclusive child care programs — or had successfully passed that energy on to their successors. I hoped they were continuing to transform how we think about, and practice, inclusion.

I revisited the ten centres.This time I traveled with three highly trained observers (Dixie Mitchell, Leona Howard, and Sherri Woitte) — one with me in each centre visited. I was particularly interested to find out how each centre had coped — to see how each had maintained or expanded or possibly lost the thread of their commitment to inclusion over the past decade. I wanted to know how centres devoted to inclusion fared in the face of changes in leadership, and what factors had facilitated or impeded their continued success.

This kind of follow-up study has rarely been undertaken. To my knowledge, the only other study that looked at these questions regarding inclusive child care programs was that of Peck, Chase Furman & Helmstetter (1993).[1]

While I talked with the director, the observer spent full days looking at the centre itself, using three instruments to measure centre quality — the *Early Childhood Environment Rating Scale – Revised (ECERS-R)*,[2] the *SpeciaLink Inclusion Practices Profile*[3] and the *SpeciaLink Inclusion Principles* Scale[4]. This contributed measures, of both overall quality and inclusion quality, that had been unavailable for the earlier visits. You can read about them in the Afterword by Donna S. Lero.

Best of all, these *Voices* give good, readable stories — extremely personal and well-informed narratives of the struggle to create learning environments for *all* children, typical as well as those with special needs — and keeping those settings alive. While there are successes, this book includes *Voices* that once had dreams and that now have to admit to some failures. Across Canada, we don't have a universal, legislated right to inclusive child care — and thus, province by province, we have often seen the idealism that gave homes to inclusion worn away by weariness, battles and lack of supportive funding. I've seen directors cry because they could no longer risk taking on the tougher challenges of some special needs. They may now have the facilities but there is not the money for training and extra staff to carry on what their youth, strength and idealism compensated for, ten years before. This is a portrait of the real Canada....

[1] Peck, C.A., Chase Furman, G. & Helmstetter, E. (1993). Integrated early childhood programs: Research on the implementation of change in organizational contexts. In C.A. Peck, S.L. Odom & D.D. Bricker (Eds.), *Integrating young children with disabilities into community programs: Ecological perspectives on research and implementation*. MD: Paul H. Brookes.

[2] Harms, T., Clifford, R.M. & Cryer, D. (1998). *Early childhood environment rating scale, revised edition (ECERS-R)*. NY: Teachers College Press, Columbia University.

[3] Irwin, S.H. (2001). *The SpeciaLink Inclusion Practices Profile*. NS: Breton Books.

[4] Irwin, S.H. (2001). *The SpeciaLink Inclusion Principles Scale*. NS: Breton Books.

1

"Even the Teacher Couldn't Pick Him Out"

Since my initial visit in 1992, this centre has survived as a high quality inclusive program despite potentially crippling changes in provincial policy that eliminated much of its support for children with special needs. The centre has grown and now occupies three sites, in large part because expansion allows it to include more children with special needs – without compromising the balance between typically developing children and children with special needs. The current director has been there for sixteen years, starting as the Special Needs Coordinator. Of all the centres in the province only this one was singled out for its inclusion quality by all provincial informants – child care advocates, provincial child care officers, and a disability association.

Sharon Hope Irwin: Over the past ten to twelve years, how has your centre changed in terms of the inclusion of children with special needs?

Centre Director: About ten years ago, we lost an important Special Needs Grant from the province that was to the tune of $35,000 per year. We lost half in 1991 and the other half in 1992.

That grant had funded a Special Needs Coordinator who worked one-on-one and in small groups and also provided classroom support. She oversaw all the rehab and therapy that the children undertook. She didn't do the therapy, but she attended most of the therapy sessions so that she could bring reports back to the teachers. That way we had good carry-over with physiotherapy, occupational therapy, and speech therapy. She also did up daily reports for the parents, explaining what their child had worked on.

Before they cut the funding, the province did quite an involved evaluation of the program to see whether their dollars were paying off. In fact, the evaluation took a year and a half for them to complete. They interviewed every parent here – not just the parents of children with special needs, but *all* the parents and *all* the staff. They went to the schools that the children who had graduated from the integrated child care program attended, to see what their follow-through was at school and where they were, and how the teachers felt the child care program had benefited them.

The report that came back was very, very positive. The conclusion of the report was that, yes, their dollars were paying off.

But we lost the funding regardless. I don't think they were intending to keep the funding in place anyway.

We lost that funding. We were able to keep our Special Needs Coordinator on for another year after that, but then we just couldn't afford it anymore. Nevertheless, we still have an integrated program. But it's different.

The funding for children with special needs disappeared, and then it got put back into place by a different method. It has now allowed us to have support staff for children that we probably wouldn't have had ten years ago, but we don't use those support staff necessarily as one-on-one. We tend to pool the staff. Eligible children are qualified, as far as funding, depending on what their needs are, for "x" number of hours of Teacher Assistant (TA) support. In the last six years, we have started to take as much of that TA support as we can and pool it together to provide a third staff person in the classroom at all times for everyone.

Well then, how did you manage despite the loss of funding for your Special Needs Coordinator? Did you have to cut back on the kids who you included or on what you could offer them?

Now, we still have kids who have cerebral palsy and are in wheelchairs and can't sit up or feed themselves. Those children have a one-on-one support person. But we may have a child who has autism, and a child with Down Syndrome, or a child who has a mild physical disability, and we may only have one support person in there for everyone in the class.

We've arranged things so that these support staff are here for 37.5 hours a week. They are part of the team. They work on the monthly programming with the teachers. We run on a monthly basis. We have a program that covers a specific theme in the curriculum each month. We decide what we're doing in the French program and what we're doing in the swim program. We pick the crafts, songs, finger plays, stories, and vocabulary that we're planning to introduce over the next month, both in French and English.

The support staff are hired as long as we have the child that they're getting funding for in the program. But in all honesty, in the ten years since we've lost our funding, we have always had the funding to keep support staff on. There's always someone else that comes into the integrated program to fill that spot. As we've grown, opening two new sites in the last two years, some of our TAs/Support Staff have now moved into full teaching positions. So we don't have a lot of turnover.

The Support Staff's income is only what we get from Family and Community Services, and each child is allotted a set rate. If a child has an established risk, the centre gets $5,150 annually from the province to cover support staff, transportation, and any equipment needed. If the parents are receiving a child care subsidy, and if there's money left over from the $5,150, it can be used to cover the difference between the child care subsidy and our actual fee which is about $40 a month.

We make it stretch by pooling the Support Staff funding. Sometimes we have six special needs children in the class, but those children wouldn't all have established risks. The other children who have more environmental risks receive a maximum of $3,150 annually. However, the majority of those children have no money to spend on any support because the majority of those children are from low-income, single-parent families, and their money often just goes to transportation. It very rarely adds to our staffing money. The money that we are paying for our support staff comes from those children who have established risks.

Since we no longer have a Special Needs Coordinator for the program, I try to fill that role to as great an extent as possible, given my other responsibilities as Executive Director of the three child care centre sites. I meet with the teachers one hour a month to see how things are going, and then I free the teachers up for one extra hour a month so that they can leave the classroom and do some planning and some brainstorming about any concerns they have about the children in the integrated program.

I also plan and arrange all the case conferences, and we have two or three a year. A case conference includes parents, therapists (if there are any), social workers (if there are any), the Public Health Nurse, and our staff. We also have one teacher and one support staff attending. If there is a social worker involved, we have the social worker attend.

If it's about a child who has a visual or hearing impairment, we have the staff from the Special Education Authority (who provide itinerant services to children with visual and auditory impairments) attend. If we have a child with autism, there's a resource/support agency here that deals with autism, and their representative may attend. It just depends on who's involved with the particular child. If the child leaves us and goes to a babysitter, we will have the babysitter come, as well. We do these conferences for all the children with established risks and for those environmentally at-risk children whom we feel will need more carry-over when they go into school.

For children who will attend school in the autumn, we have a Transfer-to-Education Meeting in the spring. We invite people from the school that the child is going to attend to come and spend the morning with us observing the child, and then we meet right after that to discuss what is going to be needed when the child enters kindergarten. These meetings give the school teachers an opportunity to come in and observe the child so that they can figure out how the child is going to fit into *their* setting. It gives them an opportunity to ask questions of the child care teacher both in the classroom and in the meeting. With most schools, we also have the Principal attend as well as the Methods and Resource Teacher. We also invite the person from the school district who holds the purse strings.

What elements of the program have been altered because of the funding changes?

At one time, we had a formal Individual Educational Plan (IEP) that we followed for each child with a special need. We don't have that anymore. Since we lost that funding for a Special Needs Coordinator in 1992, we don't have any person who can really take the time to do that. We do informal assessments of the children and set goals in gross motor, fine motor, social and behavioural skills, self help, and so forth. We used to set very specific, individualized goals. You know, we might be working on getting the child to alternate feet when ascending and descending the stairs. Now our general goal, for gross motor, would just be to have the child participate in all activities to improve mobility. That would be about it. There may be some other specific things. We have a little boy here who's blind so, of course, we're working on introducing the Braille alphabet to him.

Whereas before we had specific IEPs, now we use the curriculum that we have created for each age group as a checklist, and that is both good and bad. Sometimes it's very positive to see where the children are compared to the other children, but for some children it's not a good thing because you realize the gap is so much greater than you hoped it would be.

Ten years ago, we didn't have the at-risk kids who are

now part of our Special Needs Program. At that time, we had less than ten children with established needs and those were children with disabilities. Out of the 58 children with special needs who now attend our three centres, about a quarter of those children are children who have environmental needs, who come from at-risk families. Some of those children have more needs than others. Some just need to be in a social environment with structure and routine and they seem to get along fine. The majority of those at-risk kids had a speech delay which would have been what initially qualified them besides coming from low-income, single-parent families or whatever the other contributing circumstances were.

In the centre with 126 children, 32 with special needs, we probably have 24 children with established disabilities (11%). There are children with cerebral palsy and children with Down Syndrome. We have a child who is blind. But we no longer have that resource person, the Special Needs Coordinator, that we had ten years ago.

There's certainly a lot more onus on the teachers to oversee things, but then we've had other things that have really improved. Our communication with parents is much better, and we put more responsibility on the parents. We have a Communication Book for each child with special needs and the teachers will send home part of the curriculum and ask the parents to fill out where they feel their child is. There may be things that parents are observing at home that we didn't observe here.

I think it's been a positive thing that the teachers have taken a more first-hand role than they did when we had our Special Needs Coordinator. But, you know, there are always costs. There are some children that benefited far greater from what we had before, but then we have so many more children here now, so more children are benefiting, but maybe not individually as much. That's really hard to measure.

But we're very careful. We could fill ourselves twice over with as many kids with special needs as we have now. We have a huge waiting list. When we were first approached about opening the other centres, that waiting list was the first thing we thought of. Both the Board and I were very interested. We had a very good program for children with special needs, but we could never offer any more spaces to any more children than we had, and we knew that. So we had children who sat on the waiting list with never any hope of ever entering our doors. When the opportunity to grow came, it opened the door for more of those children with special needs.

Have you had any impact on other child care centres in your city in terms of including kids with disabilities?

I think so. Last year, we did a series of workshops free of charge, and we asked the province to kick in some money for resources and supplies. They wanted a cost breakdown and some cost estimates and a write-up. The requirements to get $500 were so intensive that we scrapped the proposal. We kept the workshops going, but we didn't ask the government for any more money. We did the workshops as volunteers. We got some donated supplies, and then the centre kicked in a bit, and some of the other bigger centres kicked in something.

We did a workshop in each of September, October, November, February, March and April. We had a Speech Pathologist come in to talk to the participants. A child psychologist did a workshop on Time Out and Time In. We had somebody from the Special Education Authority come in to talk to us about hearing impairments and how a hearing impairment can often be mistaken for an attention deficit. We had somebody come in and talk specifically about autism and Autistic Spectrum Disorder (ASD).

These workshops were each just a couple of hours long. Everybody had to bring something to share – a craft, a song, a story, a finger play, some type of unique idea. At the end of the six sessions, we pulled it all together, photocopied it, and put it in a scrapbook. That was our idea exchange, which was a really nice collaboration. We had a little certificate at the end of the workshops, too.

Everybody really enjoyed getting together. At the beginning of each session, we got everybody to stand up and say what centre they were from and how many children with special needs were involved in their program, what their main reason for attending was, and what their biggest concern was, positive and negative, in child care. So that was really neat because we don't have a lot of opportunities where we all get together. It was well attended. There were centres that we hadn't even heard of, and people came from miles away.

What do you think would happen to the quality and presence of inclusion in your centres were you to leave? Do you think it could continue?

Yes, I do. This has been my life for sixteen years, but I've left three times to have children. Last time, I was out for a year, and we arranged before I left for somebody to do what I was doing. Our current Board is very pro-integration, and we have a Special Needs Committee on our Board.

In the past, we had two years of a Board that hindered things. That was disastrous. Our Board now is all volunteer parents. Our current president is an Interventionist with Early Intervention so, of course, that's her background as well. Prior to her, the president of our Board was the parent of a child with special needs. Before that we had a speech and language pathologist. So it seems like we have very often had quite a chunk of our Board either have children with special needs or involved with children with special needs beyond just being parents. So they've always been very supportive, and we have a very positive reputation for our work with children with special needs. The Board has enjoyed that pride in what they do.

Anything new that we feel will benefit the children in general, they're very supportive of. When it comes to training, the majority of our money (and even when we didn't have any training money) has always been focused on the children with special needs. Now we have six staff doing a sign language course because this year we have three kids with cochlear implants. These kids are 9-, 10- and 14-month-olds. So, for the staff working with them, we're introducing sign language in order to enhance the language skills that those kids are getting.

As for the money that has come out of our own coffers for training, 99% of it has been because we have a child with a special need, or a unique situation where we really need to have somebody trained in order to provide a child with what we want to provide. The Board's Special Needs Committee has worked with me on the proposals to get some of our grant and foundation money. We would do up a proposal to get support for a specific child, or a specific disability. The Board has always been very supportive and involved in that.

What aspects of your program are you most proud of?

Our Board and parents would probably be the most proud of our staff. We have very little turnover. Ninety-nine percent of the staff would go to the ends of the earth and dedicate any amount of time in order to better serve the children. We have had the occasional person who didn't like to participate in anything after hours, but very few have felt that way.

When monies have been limited, the staff has been really good at coming up with ideas and activities that would be low cost. We can send one staff member to a workshop and that person will come back and give the rest of the staff a training session on what they've learned.

I'm sure you're not going to find too many centres that have staff that have been there 26 years. We have two people who have been here that long. Both these staff have B.Eds, so they could probably have gone elsewhere for more money long ago, but they didn't.

We do pay more than most other child care centres in this city. Eighty-six percent of our revenue pays staff. Still, we don't pay well, but then no child care centre pays well. We start at $8.20 an hour, but we also have Blue Cross Benefits, and we have a few other little perks. When we don't have money, our Board finds other ways to make everybody feel valued.

At Christmas, the regular staff here doesn't work for a period of a week or two. We have support staff and relief staff whom the children are familiar with come in so that the teachers get a break and are paid over that time. We also have a Teacher Appreciation Day, and the food and the gifts are unbelievable. The Board coordinates all of that. It is a great place to work! We all have our ups and downs, but there is no one here that can say they don't feel valued by our Board.

Are there any contradictions between the Applied Behavioural Analysis (ABA)* experiences some specialists promote for kids with autism with your apparently play-based child care centre programs?

That's a hot topic here, as I'm sure it is everywhere, because everybody's pushing to have somebody who's ABA trained. The interventionists with the autism program who support our autistic children one-on-one aren't all ABA trained. For those children with autism, they actually have assumed the role that our Special Needs Coordinator once played, but only for those children with autism.

We're getting lots of support for the autistic children from the autism program, both in the classroom and outside of the classroom. They may work at the back or in a quiet corner of the classroom, and they may work in the classroom with a group. It depends on what the child needs. We have some children under the Autism Spectrum Disorder (ASD) umbrella who socialize quite well and can work in the classroom, and then we have other children for whom any noise is a distraction and their ability to weed out the irrelevant information coming at them is just not there, so those kids would be removed from the classroom at times.

Is there a story that deals with a particular child or situation in the daycare centre that, for you, is illustrative of how your program works?

---

* Applied Behavioural Analysis (ABA), sometimes called Intensive Behavioural Intervention (IBI), is a well-known therapy used with children witih autism.

"Even the Teacher Couldn't Pick Him Out"

I often go back to one of my earliest experiences. This child is now 22 years old. This took place during my first year working here when my first group of children was leaving the centre to go to school.

Back then, there was no public kindergarten in our province, just Grade One. We did our Transfer-to-Education Meetings and had the school teachers come in to observe a child who was going in to Grade One the next year. A Methods and Resource teacher and a teacher's aide had come because this child was going to need a teacher's aide. This little boy, Ben, had global developmental delay, ADHD, and a significant speech delay. He had delays in all areas. He was probably functioning more at the three-year level when he was actually six years old.

Anyway, when I took the visiting teachers into the classroom, the class was having circle time, and I said, "Well, Ben is there in the circle."

And they said, "Well, we'll just sit and watch."

"Well, do you want me...?"

"Oh, no, no. We'll be able to pick him out; no problem."

So they sat down there. An hour later, I went back. They had finished circle and story time. They had done their calendar and the days of the week. They had done their songs and finger plays. They'd done a craft, and they were getting ready for outdoor play.

I asked how things were going and reminded the visitors that we were going to start the meeting in about a half hour or so. I said, "Have you had a chance to observe Ben a lot?"

"Yes, he is quite busy."

I said, "He has his moments, but he's come leaps and bounds," and we talked about this child for a few minutes. Then they stood up and they said, "Good bye, Ben" – to a little boy by the name of Kelsey who didn't have any disability!

I said, "That's not Ben!" and they were shocked. They had observed the wrong child for an hour. I thought that really says something about our program that this child fits into the program so well that the Methods and Resource teacher, the teacher's aide, and the teacher couldn't even pick him out.

Has your vision of inclusion changed in any way?

At the preschool level, no. Beyond that, yes. I have a stepson who has special needs. Actually, my stepson is Ben, the child I was just telling you about. He wasn't my stepson then, but he is now. I didn't even know his father back then but, eight years after I worked with Ben, I met his dad. It's funny how things changed.

When Ben was in child care, and even in elementary school, integration in all aspects of the school program worked for him. When it came time for him to go to middle school and junior high, I saw firsthand that integration doesn't work for every child at those levels. When he started middle school, Ben segregated himself because, socially, he didn't fit in with the other children at all. The group that he chose socially was other children with disabilities.

I still came across many other parents of children with special needs who were saying, "I want my child in that regular social studies class," and that child was functioning at a five-year-old level and getting I don't know what out of social studies. I thought, "Why would we bother having a child sit in that classroom for 90 minutes when he could benefit from something involving more daily living skills?" It was always a big question to me why would we continue to include children who don't fit in and don't want to be included. As they get older, some of these kids with special needs want to have their own peer group as all teenagers do.

My thoughts about integration changed with regard to teens because Ben made it very clear to me that integration wasn't what met his needs anymore. When Ben was in high school, he had an English Literature course that was doing Shakespeare. It was *Romeo and Juliet*. Shakespeare's English is hard enough for us to understand, never mind a child who is functioning ten years behind and has a language delay. So I bought the "Wishbones" book. I don't know if you remember "Wishbones." He is a little dog, and he takes roles in history and makes the stories more accessible at the child's level. Anyway, I bought a "Wishbone" book, and we did *Romeo and Juliet* at Ben's level, and that worked for us.

At the preschool level, I'm still a believer in integrating and including special needs children in all aspects of preschool education. And even, as I said, in the elementary years. But I think we need to do more individualized programming for some kids at the high school level. I think at times we get lost in, "Everybody needs to be integrated all the time." That doesn't work for everybody. Some children would benefit from three music classes in a day rather than sitting in Language Arts. And I think, as I said, parents get so caught up in, "I want my child doing... ." Now some children fit into everything, don't get me wrong. I think some modification of programs works well for lots of kids, but there are some things that can't be modified to meet some children's needs. I think then integration goes in the wrong direction, as far as I'm concerned.

What is your wish list for the child care centres? Your wish list 12 years ago was about the playground.

We got that playground, but now we have to take that playground down because it's made of pressure-treated lumber. We have until 2006 to get rid of it. We have new playground equipment coming, but our playground equipment right now is all wheelchair accessible. The new playground equipment that we have so far is not accessible at all. The playground we have right now is wonderful but, as I said, it has got to go. We've decided to go with heavy-duty, lasts forever, plastic stuff this time, and we may have to look at putting in cedar ramps.

As for my current wish list, I would love to have that rubber matting stuff that costs an arm and a leg all over the flooring of the playground. We looked at a little piece of it last year for a very small area. Fifteen by forty was $26,000, but it is wonderful stuff for all children and, for our kids with special needs, it would've been the greatest asset that we could have added to allow them more mobility.

I would love to have equipment for more speech and language programming for our computers. We got a touch window years ago for our computer, but now there are all kinds of adapted equipment that you can use with the computer for the kids. More computers would be great, too.

We would also love to have a Braille writer. That costs about $6,000. We have this little guy here who is only just four. He's our first child who is completely blind. He doesn't see shadows or anything. We have two staff members who are learning to read and write Braille, so we're starting to introduce the alphabet and would like him to recognize his name and other simple words and know all the letters before he goes to school in the fall. He is just one bright little cookie. I mean, you could come into that classroom and say, "Hi, Dylan," and tell him who you are, and talk to him for a few minutes and come back next month, and he'd say, "Oh, that's Lillian." He just blows us away. Bright, bright cookie.

In terms of human resources wishes, I would like to re-introduce our Special Needs Coordinator. That would certainly be supportive, but we would need two or three people now in order to meet those needs. We would love, *love* to have a speech and language pathologist on staff because that certainly is the commonality. Whether it's a child with an established need or a kid with an environmental need, 95% of them have language concerns. Expressive language or receptive language or major problems with pronunciation, so many have language problems.

We could certainly use more rooms in our centre. We have nowhere to go. Our gym has now become our after-school room out of sheer need. But we do have a resource room for the teachers, which is now internet accessible, and the teachers use that a fair amount of time. We also have a staff room.

What else would I like? You know, if you asked me this last year, I would have said we'd love to have a van, but we have a van now, which we purchased in July. Still, we could certainly use another one already!

Are there kids with any level or type of disability that you feel apprehensive about including?

No. None. We had a little girl with spina bifida who was

no problem to include. She is bright as a button. Her Mom wanted us to catheterize her because she had no sensation from the waist down and, of course, that was a big issue. "Whoa! What do we do with this child?" Our biggest concern, of course, was hurting the little girl.

So instead, we had the nursing students from the university come over every day for three weeks and teach seven staff how to do catheterization so we always had back-up. The Board had a big discussion to ensure that it wasn't going to be done in the classroom even though we had bathrooms in the classroom. It was not something that we wanted children to have questions about. Anyway, once we got past those three weeks, we then had four other children who required catheterization as the years progressed, and now we wouldn't blink twice at that.

We had that little guy here who had a G-tube, a J-tube, and a tracheotomy that was suctioned every hour or so. He'd go through moments where he sounded like he was taking his last gasp, but the suctioning just became old hat to us after a while.

When he went to school, they hired a nurse. We couldn't get anything like that here so, again, we fell back on the university's nursing students who came in and talked us through it daily until we were comfortable. We trained a number of people just in case someone was out sick or in an emergency. We did it fine for a year and a half, and then he went to school, and they said, "No, not without a nurse," and the funding came. We have to cope, but the schools don't ever have to cope! They always seem to kind of come up with funds from somewhere for schools, but anyway, he fared fine with us.

Each time we introduce someone like that, when we conquer that battle and actually make progress with that child who has a very unique need, I always feel a huge sense of pride. It's another feather in our cap that we can say that we have staff that have been there, done that. And I know our Board have always felt that way, and everybody in this city knows that, if there's a child who has a need that no other place can serve, we always will.

What about your typically developing kids and your kids who are gifted, do you think they lose out with your focus on special needs?

Absolutely not. First of all, if we can modify a program to meet a child who has a delay, we can certainly modify a program for a child who is gifted or advanced. The staff/child ratio in the classroom benefits everybody. The Support Staff are there *because* we have children with special needs, but the ratio benefits *all* the children.

Certainly, we've *always* felt that having children that have unique needs benefits the garden variety children. I mean, we've introduced sign language and Braille to children who would never have had opportunities to learn those things. We've never— knock on wood – *never* had a parent have an issue with any of that. We've never had a parent who said, "Hey, wait. Now why are you signing a book in the classroom? My child doesn't need sign language." We've had parents come into the office and say, "My child keeps signing (and they'll do a sign), what does that mean? Can I have a list of those signs because he's using them regularly?" All parents have been very supportive of that.

Parents have also been very conscious when it comes to birthday parties and things like that to include the children in the classroom who have special needs. Parents often come into the classroom and say things like, "I know Debbie is in a wheelchair, but do you think her mother would be comfortable with coming to a party at the bowling alley?" Knowing Debbie's parents, we can respond, "Mom would be thrilled, and Debbie will have a great time. She'd love to be around the other kids."

I think it has certainly enhanced the lives not only of the children here, but of the parents who have become far more aware. These are parents who went through the school system and didn't see many children with special needs because those children were segregated in special education programs. You would think at times we would have parents say, "Hmm, I'm not altogether comfortable with this," but we haven't ever had that. I think we've never had that because our teachers are so accepting. We do have the proper support to have those kids included, and the parents know that.

When we have new parents come in, we always say, "We are a very large integrated centre." That's the first thing. "We have a large number of children with special needs here. We do sign language with the kids because we have children that are hearing impaired here. We have a ramp here because we have children that have physical disabilities. We have this fridge here because we have children that have extra dietary needs." We'll go through all that when we do the tour of the centre. Everything speaks of integration.

Even for parents of a child who doesn't have a special need, every second sentence out of our mouths is, "Well, we have five staff in here and four staff in there, because we have children with special needs. And when we have a child with exceptional needs, we'll often put in extra support so that all the children benefit from that child being in the classroom. At our circle and story time in all the centres, we have a little music stand because that's where the book goes so the teachers can sign and read at the same time."

I've never had anyone say, "Well, I'm not really comfortable having my child in that class with that child who has all the tubes, but thank you anyway." It's always been more like, "Isn't that wonderful?"

My kids all came through here. We also have three staff here who are adults with exceptional needs. Two of them were here as preschoolers before my time. We have a 27-year-old young lady with Down Syndrome who has been a classroom assistant here for the last seven years. We also have a young lady who works in our kitchen who has special needs, and we have another person with special needs who comes in part-time to help with our four-year-old group downstairs. So, you see, we try to practice what we preach.

2

"No More Pull-Outs"

Through the 1980s and early 1990s, this centre was viewed as one of the most inclusive in Canada, attracting visitors and students from all provinces and even other countries. The current director, who started here as an ECE practicum student, has continued to anchor inclusion into the second generation. For her, inclusion is a given and, despite increasing regulatory and practice barriers that defy informal solutions, she sees that children with special health needs and other challenging care needs are welcomed – even if she must take on direct service roles herself. She has succeeded in making "no pull-outs" the norm.

On the downside, however, where once the building was viewed as an innovative inclusive structure, it is now outdated and requires immediate replacement. The director reports that some staff have lost their earlier "we can do it" approach to inclusion. While it was the only centre recommended as a successful inclusionary center in 1991 by all three provincial informants – that would not likely be the case today.

Sharon Hope Irwin: Over the past ten to twelve years, how has your centre changed with regards

to the inclusion of children with special needs?

Centre Director: In 1977, when I was finishing high school and uncertain about further education directions, I went to a career fair. At first, I thought the woman with the pet gerbil was a veterinarian. Intrigued, I watched as she put up her table among the other displays for careers such as teaching, police work and law. Her display had lots of pictures of children engaged in all sorts of activities – and the gerbil. I started talking with the woman, and learned that she had recently started a child care centre in our town. I had always gravitated towards children – and when babysitting, always wanted to do activities with them. But until this centre opened, there was no child care centre in our town. The gerbil lady told me all about the program and the opportunities for employment. She also told me about a new two-year Early Childhood Education (ECE) training program at the teachers' college five hours drive away. And that was it – I never looked back.

In addition to demonstrating child-centred activities at Career Fairs by including live gerbils, the founding director of our centre was passionate about the inclusion of children with special needs. From my first visit to the centre (while I was still in high school), I saw these children included. Although my ECE training did not include "special needs," I was mentored in this area during my practicum placements at this centre and during the 15 years I worked there, as a frontline staff, before I became director.

So one huge change has been that our founding director, who had been here since the centre opened fifteen years earlier, left for another job. She was the woman with the gerbil who hooked me on working in child care. I succeeded her as director and to me it was just natural to feel that all children had a right to be included and could be included.

One other thing that has changed is that therapists here in the community have become more involved. Instead of traveling hundreds of miles to the children's hospital in this province, children are receiving more of their services here in their local community, so that has certainly changed things for us.

The communication with the children's treatment providers has really evolved. Now we are working directly with various outside professionals, meeting with speech therapists, physiotherapists, and anyone else involved in caring for a child who attends our centre.

Another important change is that "pull-outs" are no longer something that our child care centre does. Ideally, it's all group work, and we move toward that. Starting about ten years ago, we moved away from doing pull-outs and toward having things done in a more natural setting. What we're working on now is getting the various professionals who come here to see the value in doing things that way.

When a specialist comes in to see a child, we want that person to go in and play with the child in the housekeeping corner, or to join them at the art table, or to join them at small group time. That way, they are going to see more of what that child is doing, and they get a chance to talk with the staff in the room and see what's going on and what some of their concerns are.

Working right in the classroom is especially important when helping kids with autism. I think that's *so* important. It's *so* unnatural for those kids to go up into a separate room to meet. Sometimes, when there's testing that has to be done, that's a different situation, and it has to been done separately, but mostly we want the children to remain with their class.

Even last year, some of the professionals – the occupational therapist and the speech therapists – hadn't gotten that. When they came in, they were pulling the kids out. I don't know what they were hoping to see in that little room. I really don't. Most of the time, even in the group setting, the kids will cooperate and will sit and do puzzles and things on a one-on-one basis – things the therapists want to see.

The specialists need to come and see what the kids do and how they do it when they're in their natural setting. And now they're seeing that. They are finally getting it. Some of these therapists have attended workshops with child care people and that helped them see the value of group work.

There is a provincial special needs review going on now, so the therapists were a part of the meetings that discussed the concept of this funding, how it came into play, and how they want child cares to use this funding. So they were a part of those discussions, and they spent some time with us at those meetings. Specialists are starting to see that when they come in to the centre, it's important to talk to the staff and see how kids play and learn in the regular setting.

A couple of the kids here have private speech therapy, and the speech therapist comes and takes the child out of the classroom because they're working on specific things. And that's fine, I mean, that's here. It is better that it takes place here in the surroundings that they're used to, instead of them going elsewhere – such as to a clinic in the hospital. It still works best when there is communication with child care staff about the child's progress. The specialists give us ideas that we can incorporate into circle time or into small group time, too.

What else has changed?

I think that the staff's response to taking on a new child with special needs has changed.

The staff now get far more information about a child before that child comes into the centre than we used to get. Because of these reports before meeting the child, the staff sometimes feel more pressured at the outset. When I was a teacher in the unit, if we had a new child, I thought, "OK, we have this child. What kinds of things do we need to have in place to include this child?" Now I find some staff experience added stress when a new child starts – especially where a child is said to have really challenging behaviour – and I am more pressured to have an extra pair of hands available.

Before, we would work with what we already had in place in terms of resources in the room. We did something. We took turns. It was just expected of us. Now, I find we're more pressured – and this is probably because we know more about the child before the child comes. So, if the staff perceives that a child is going to have really, really challenging behaviours because, for example, the child is in the zero-to-three years home-based Early Intervention Program – they are on the director right away to give them extra support even before the child comes to child care.

Our door has always been open to kids with special needs, and it's not so much that we are taking more kids with special needs, it's how we take kids now that has changed. The staff is more a part of that process, and we talk more about the kids before they come to us. Ten years ago, there wasn't a whole lot of opportunity to sit down before the child came into our care and talk with all these different professionals about the child. The director and the resource coordinator held that responsibility in the past.

Now more people are involved in intake because of programs like Early Intervention. The more involvement you get, the more you know about the child early in the process, and then there are concerns about our capacity to include the child before the child comes. I have found that this involvement and discussion before the child comes to the centre can lead to labeling and can sometimes even create preconceptions and barriers.

Having more people involved works both ways though, and it can be a positive thing. Now, when we get a child in the centre who needs special care beyond what we are capable of giving, we can go to outside resources and pull in other people. For example, a couple of years ago, we wanted to include a child who required special feeding techniques. The child's needs were beyond what we were trained to do in terms of feeding. While we were looking for a way to make it work, we found that someone had been going into the child's home to do some of this feeding for the Mom. We were able to have that same person who provided respite care for the family come here to the centre at mealtime so that staff felt comfortable. I find you have to tap into resources like that, and we are better able to do that now than we were before.

What about the types of kids you are taking?

That really hasn't changed. It still depends on the children we have on our waiting list and the families that are looking for child care.

At present, we have a little girl coming who has Down Syndrome and has feeding difficulties. She has a feeding tube. Her Mom isn't comfortable with leaving her here for the whole day because she is still tube fed at home, but we're hoping that, by next year, she will be able to stay longer and have the full day. That means we're going to have to really have everything that's required in place beforehand.

We're getting more children with different challenges but, as far as the kids that we're taking, it varies from year to year and depends on what children are on our waiting list.

Have you had any impact on other child care centres in your city in terms of including kids with disabilities?

Yes. Right from the beginning (1976) we knew that we could never accommodate all the children with special needs whose parents wanted them in our program. We knew that if we enrolled them all, we would have a segregated centre, since all (or almost all) of our children would have special needs or environmental at-risk issues.

So, as I understand it, by 1979, our centre sponsored an outreach program that provided staffing support to other centres that would include children with special needs as well as an itinerant resource teacher to help the other centres develop individualized programs and positive attitudes toward inclusion. We were even able to provide a range of resources, including equipment and modest modifications to classrooms.

About ten years later, the provincial government agreed to fund extra supports to all centres, on a child by child basis, so we no longer had to find grants to support these outreach staff.

But we are still seen as the leader in inclusion in our region, and continue to advise and consult when asked. Our outreach program became a funded Early Intervention program and it has taken on much of the consulting role to other centres. Still, on a director-to-director basis, I am frequently asked to help solve problems and make suggestions.

Do you think inclusion would survive if you left the program?

That's a hard question! I don't really know. I guess it would depend on who took my place. In order for inclusion to work, the director, the staff, the Board, everyone involved has to embrace inclusion. That's what we were taught, and I keep going back to that. We were very lucky because we started in a centre that embraced inclusion. It was just something natural to do.

I think that, if somebody here on staff took over my position, inclusion would continue. Some things might change. The number of children with special needs in the classrooms would be something they would look at changing. I think you would see numbers in the classrooms decrease.

I have been really challenged in my thinking and in everything that I believe in. For example, at the end of the day, I realize that the child is attached to a family. If we take a child with special needs whose parent is working, that parent has to have the same hours free as any other parent who's out working. If the child with special needs is not able to cope as long in a child care setting, we still have to realize that the child isn't just here because he has special needs; he is also here because Mom is working, and we have to find a way to make the longer day work. The whole family's needs have to be considered.

Those are the kinds of things I would be worried about, that they could get lost.

When someone else takes over, the commitment will change. It will still be strong, but in a different way. I don't think it could stay the same.

My philosophy is that you have to go above and beyond to make it happen. We have got to find a way to make it work. If you've got that child in your centre, then you've got to do the best job that you can do to make that work. I think child cares are getting lost now in all these various policies. Don't get me wrong – I think policies are important – but with some of these policies, we get so caught up in rules and requirements, licensing and that kind of stuff, that people just don't want to do it anymore.

What role does your Board play in maintaining the commitment to inclusion?

When I came on, I brought a strong commitment to inclusion, and I think the Board has embraced that. For the two years between our founding director's leaving and my becoming director, there were a few concerns about the view that all kids can be included in school – there was less commitment to inclusion. We were starting to run into problems with school principals. We had conversations about whether we should be pushing inclusion in the school. Were we expecting too much from the children? Are the teachers and the schools able to include all kids? Are our expectations too great? Just from reading old minutes, I can see we talked about those issues at different Board meetings, but I feel that the current Board is pretty open to what I've been working for. I haven't had any difficulty with the Board.

If we feel strongly about something, I bring it to the

Board. They might have their opinions but, at the end of the day, they see that it's working for us, and we feel it's going to continue to work. I find the Board very open to our vision as to what children the child care centre can include. I've never had any difficulties with an opinion of the Board about children that we wanted to take. They might have questions. How is that going to impact on the other children? How is that going to impact on the program? How are you going to make it work? But they are very supportive of what we're doing.

When you think of your successes in maintaining and promoting inclusion, what have been some of the hurdles or barriers that you have managed to deal with?

Trying to balance our after-school program has been a challenge. Trying to run a summer camp including kids with special needs so that they feel successful has been a challenge. And cost. That's a challenge. We did a lot of juggling this summer when the province pulled the funding for our "extra" special needs kids.

We received a call, and they said that they were over their budget. I had told the parents that, yes, we had child care spaces for them for the summer, and we had quite a few kids coming. About a week before the kids were to begin, they pulled the funding, which meant probably $10,000 for our centre.

Well, we kept the kids, and we were very lucky with how it all worked itself out. We had two excellent summer students. I don't know what we would have done without them. And I had this second person who was phenomenal. It just worked. We had a good summer. I spent some time with the school-aged kids when staff members were on vacation and stuff like that. We just juggled it and made it work. But it was hard. Losing that revenue was very difficult. That was a real challenge.

Another challenge we now face is that our second floor for our school-aged kids is not accessible. It's dangerous, and that's not acceptable. If you are carrying a child up a flight of stairs, it's not safe. That's a potential liability, too. These are things you didn't think about in the past. You just did it and that was that. But now people are conscious and thinking about those things.

Challenging behaviours are another issue we face. We need to have people in place for children who really, really need, not pull-out one on one, but an extra person to give support in the classroom to help them be included and feel successful. Where is the money going to come from?

Being a child care centre that is unionized has its challenges too. At one point, we had one particular child who was very challenging. The staff felt that they were stressed, and they felt that I wasn't doing enough. They got the union involved, and I found that very difficult. I found that hard because it's a child care centre – it's not a union matter.

It doesn't happen very often but, at times, you feel that you haven't done enough. Or you feel the staff feel that you're not respecting their work and what they are trying to do. How can we overcome that and have them trust me again? Trying to work through things with the family, and the child, and the staff all at once can be a challenge.

When you think of all the problems you have and all the things you juggle, what are the stories you keep in mind to remind yourself that it's really worth it?

Steven, a child with severe cerebral palsy – I'm telling

you, I fill up every time I think of him. He's one example. I see Steven now when he's graduating from high school, and I just feel that, if I played one tiny little part in that child being the great success that he is, then inclusion definitely is a success. Steven can't move independently, use his hands or speak, but it is obvious that he is very, very bright. He came to the centre when he was less than 2 years old, and right from the start, the other kids included him in everything. Not because he was needy in some way, but because they saw that beyond his disability was another little kid with a great sense of humour and a lot of ideas.

There's an example of a family that just wanted their child to be with other children. They just wanted him to be a little boy. That's all they were looking for. When they came here, they weren't looking for our developmental program. They were working. They needed child care, and they wanted Steven to be with other children.

When I think of him in the classroom and the things that he did.... We often talk about it. Every time I look at the videos and pictures of him working in small group, I just...I don't know. And, he's not the only one. There are lots of other kids who have gone through the program who have inspired me, but Steven is one who will always stay with me.

I also think of Mitchell who was gifted. One day, I got out a book that I had written and filled with notes on different things about children. I had kept a copy of Mitchell's social assessment; and, today, he is like that assessment predicted he would be. When he went off to school, I said to his parents, "He really needs to get in a classroom where he's going to be challenged. He's really not going to like kindergarten. He looks at things in a different way, and he needs somebody to see that he's not acting out. He's still a little boy, but he is one who looks at things differently." And when I ran into them later? Sure enough. Mitchell *hated* kindergarten. I often think of him.

There have been a lot of kids who went through our program and were involved with kids with special needs, and everybody was challenged in different ways. I think of all those kids, too.

Do you think it is of value for typically developing kids to be involved with kids with special needs?

Definitely. When you see a child helping another child by zippering up their jacket, and taking them by the hand and helping them, you know that child has been watching what we're doing and knows that the other child might do things in a different way.

The children pick things up from the teachers. I know one little guy who had the teacher helping him with the scissors when they were doing a cutting project. She left him for a few minutes. When she came back, another little girl wanted to do the cutting with him. Things like that.

I think it's wonderful when you see the children interacting with each other, and it's so natural in a setting like this in a way that it wouldn't be if you were pulling kids out all the time. It's because the kids are included that you see those kinds of things happening. The children benefit, both children with disabilities and typically developing kids.

How has your vision of inclusion changed over the years?

I still believe that all kids should be included, no matter

what their disability. I am just more realistic. It's not that my vision has changed, but how I approach it has. I'm not as naïve. I know that certain things have to be in place for inclusion to work.

You can't just say, "These are the kids we're taking." You have to think, "Are we going to have to change the classroom? What kinds of things will we need?" For instance, when Jack came, he was totally visually impaired, and we had never worked with a child who was visually impaired to that degree, so we had to have some training for the staff, and we had to rearrange the classroom.

It wasn't until the first time I walked into this child care centre to do my training placement here that I got any real exposure to kids with special needs. I remember, after being here for about three weeks, saying to a staff member one day, "This little guy does some different little things…." I remember he used to rock back and forth for long periods of time. I didn't realize that he was autistic. I'd never heard of that. I never questioned why he was there at the centre. I just thought that was a natural thing that this centre did.

I was lucky to be here from the very beginning and to be part of how it grew. Being a part of all that has certainly helped me to develop my attitude toward inclusion.

If you could go back to when you took over as director, and you could do it all again, are there any things you would do differently?

I'd put to use the things I've learned along the way. For example, I've learned over the years to make sure that, as the director, I am involved in all aspects of the process. I can't just rely on the Special Needs Coordinator to collect all the information. I can't take for granted that people are going to look at things the way that I look at them. I have to be involved.

I have also learned that transitions are important and to make sure that all the outside people involved in helping a child make a transition communicate to the staff.

What is your wish list for the centre?

A new facility. A brand new centre with many bright, big rooms and open spaces. The rooms should have good observation spots with speakers like the ones I've seen elsewhere. That would really assist us in showing how this works. I think that having places where teachers and therapists and parents can look at the class and hear what's happening would be very valuable.

I wish we had big spaces for the kids to work on gross motor skills right in the class. I also wish we had more small rooms and extra people. The kids would benefit because we could have more programs going on at one time. If somebody wanted to take four or five kids and go into the gym or into a break-out room and do something, they could. We could do more small group things.

For teachers, working in very small groups is important because you can see where the kids are. You're interacting more. When everybody is together all of the time, it's a little more difficult to interact meaningfully and assess a particular child's progress and needs. Right now we don't have the staff or the space to do as much small group work as I would like.

Better space would also help with getting families more involved in the programming by making it possible for families to spend more time at the centre if they wanted to. Not that they can't now, but having the time and space built in so that the families could become more involved in all the planning would be wonderful.

I wish for new computers for the classrooms. That's what we're aiming for now. I'd like to have computer centres built into each classroom.

I also wish we could afford to attend lots of new training and to spend lots of time meeting and planning. It would be great if we could have time built in for staff to get together with the lead teachers, with the director and with the Special Needs Coordinator. Having that planning time is *so* important

Being able to afford all of these things for our centre – that would be my dream.

3

"Trying to Take Inclusion on the Road"

Located in a large metropolitan children's hospital, this exceptionally fine example of an earlier model of inclusion was "grandfathered" to continue to accept up to 50% children with special needs when the province implemented its new maximum ratio of one child with special needs to eight typically developing children. Centres such as this one make us doubt the wisdom of rigidity in inclusion proportions – at least in a time of limited funding and resources. They enroll children with the most severe disabilities, children that most other centres are still afraid to take. We witnessed a session led by a dance therapist that included four children with differing, severe special needs. The staff skillfully accommodated and modified for these children's full participation in the "Hokey-pokey" and other routines. The other children seemed completely comfortable with the activity, and the adults enjoyed it as well.

As more centres move toward full inclusion, staff from this centre will be critically needed as trainers, consultants and coaches, and centres such as this one will be needed as models – offering inclusive practicum placements for ECE students.

The director and Special Needs Coordinator of this centre have already tried to promote their vision of inclusion to community-based centres through an Itinerant Resource Teacher model – but take-up wasn't sufficient, and that funding stopped.

Sharon Hope Irwin: How does inclusion work in this centre?

Centre Director: I have been with this child care centre for thirteen years. Most of that time was spent working as an Early Childhood Educator (ECE). For the past four years, my role has been that of Special Needs Coordinator. The director created my position in order to implant a support so that the child care centre could integrate more fully.

I'm the connection between all the therapists and the ECEs in the classrooms. I work with occupational therapists, physiotherapists, speech language specialists and a play therapist. I take everything they tell me about their work with a child – for example, the objectives they are working toward in therapy – and I tell the ECEs so we can work on the same things here.

We are not to the stage where the therapists come here. They may come to observe, but they do the therapy one-on-one elsewhere. It's all because of insurance and stuff like that. That's why I act as the connection between the therapists and the staff at the centre.

But for me, therapy just one-on-one doesn't click. I find the children need at least one other child there to model behaviours. We as adults can do some modeling, but we're not at the same level, and it is not as effective as working around other children.

I do little group sessions. I take certain kids out of the class with one friend to come into my office and work on an objective. It's not one-on-one, but it's not in a big group, so they can focus more with me, in those little groups. It's easier for the kids to learn because they get more attention, and the "regular" kid – the friend who is involved – that friend helps, too. The child has the model of the other friend. I am not a therapist, but that's my ideal for therapy.

The children in my small groups take turns, and they carry their connection back into the classroom. The kids are all really close in the class, and they help each other a lot. They know, "Her, she can't talk. No, you have to speak with signs." They know, because we talk about it. "She can't hear. Why?" They ask questions, and we try to answer. We hide nothing.

If there's a kid who signs, when we do circle time with the story and songs, we have to sing with signs. All the kids at the end of the year sing "Good Morning" with the signs. Most of the kids are bilingual because they deal with French and English all the time. And sometimes they leave with the sign language, too. It depends on whether there is a hearing impaired child in the class. If there is, they catch the words because we use sign language all the time. The only child who's not leaving bilingual is a child who has some intellectual deficiencies. We have to stick with just one language with that child.

My work is related to three classrooms that work in both French and English. We are a regular child care, but we have a larger concentration of children with disabilities. Out of sixty full-time children, twenty-four have special needs. I believe we are the only centre of this kind in the province. Most of the kids come five days a week. We accept two days to five. We don't accept one day per week attendance because, for us, we can't see the progress. So we start at two days. We really prefer three days per week attendance for the kids. They get more friendship, more continuity, and more understanding of routines when they are here more often.

We don't have kids with autism integrated yet. We tried in the past, but it was really hard because they really need one-on-one. So, after three or four experiences, we feel that we can't meet their needs. It's not that we don't want to have them here, but it didn't work. We tried to direct them to another place (a specialized treatment centre) that we know.

How did your travelling resource teacher program work?

I used to travel as a resource teacher and do consultations so that is how I began providing support to staff in child cares. With that traveling program, teachers would call and talk about the problems that they had in their centres and the needs they had. They set appointments with me, starting with three sessions. I would go in there and observe for the first session. I talked a little bit with the teacher, and I looked at the classroom and at the child or children whose needs we were considering.

On the second visit, I would bring examples of appropriate activities. I met with the teacher, and I talked about my observations, and I gave her some ideas. I never told her what to do because that was not my job. I was just there to help. I was an ECE before so it was easy for me to understand what their problems were. For example, most of the teachers didn't know how to adapt an activity for a visually impaired kid. I have some practical experience in a child care centre working with special needs, so I had that to offer.

The third visit was to follow up after the teacher had a chance to try some of the suggested activities. We would usually wait one month before I made my third visit. It depended. Sometimes they would call up and say, "Please come back," earlier, but we would try one month, and they could call me during that period for help.

When I did the traveling job, I often heard, "This place is not adapted for that kind of kid. We had one experience and it was so negative that we do not want to do it anymore because there's no help." A lot of the kids weren't diagnosed so the teacher just looked and said, "I think something's not right with that kid," so they called us. But we're not therapists, so we just tried to direct them to call the right person and get on a waiting list for evaluation.

That travelling resource service just wasn't used enough, so we stopped that program. I think it ended in 1995, around there. Despite the end to that program, our goal is still to expand the number of centres that are prepared to include kids with disabilities. The teachers are good observers, but they still don't know where to turn for diagnoses and help. Too often, when they knock at the door, it's closed. We're working on a book of contact people, a directory of resources for the teachers to start with.

What happened when the travelling resource program closed?

When the travelling program closed, I went from being a travelling resource teacher to being the internal Special Needs Coordinator here. The director found the money to create this position. The inclusion thinking was just starting to take root.

Pre-diagnosis, we just offer what we can to the children in our centre who aren't getting the therapy they need. In each class in the child care centre, there's a Human Services worker who studied to work with all kinds and ages of people with physical and intellectual challenges. So in each class, we try to have two trained staff, one of whom has been trained as an Early Childhood Educator and one of whom is a Human Services worker. You don't have that in a regular child care setting. Our ratio is usually 2 adults for 12 children. We have one big class of 17 this year, and that class has 3 staff plus a student. We have a lower child-to-staff ratio than other centres in this city in recognition of the proportion of kids with disabilities.

Our centre is physically accessible because we're on one floor. A lot of the kids on the waiting list have physical disabilities, and other child care centres can't accommodate them because they are not accessible. At the other child cares in the city, most of the integrated kids have speech or intellectual delays, but not physical disabilities.

One of our children, Raymond, has a lot of equipment to help with mobility, and he's heavy so you can't carry him. He needs to be in the classes on the first floor. Right now he's in with the infants. It would be easiest to keep him in that class, but that's not what we want for him. Here, the way we work, every kid is in their age group. Even if a child is at six months intellectually, he's going to be in with the four-year-olds because that's his group.

Our work is to adapt everything for him, and ensure that he sees the behaviour of other four-year-old girls and boys. Even if, when we meet with the parents they say,

"No, no, no. Don't put my kid with…." This is how it works here. At the beginning, the parents may be scared, but most of them eventually think it's a good idea. They see that it is what is best for the child. If they are going to grow, that's what they need.

We try to give the most that we can, you know. Give the opportunity to all the kids to participate. Even for the ones who have intellectual challenges, we adapt our activities to include them.

What about the parents of typically developing children. Do any of those parents ever feel that their children are being ignored or overlooked?

No, because when they come and register their kids they know how our centre works. They know that their child is going to be next to kids with special needs. If they didn't accept that, they would go somewhere else.

A few times, we have heard parents say things like, "Now he's regressing because he looks at his friend…*blah blah blah*." In order to respond to that, we try to be real. We say, "He's going to do that for one week because he thinks it's funny, but he's going to stop," and they all stop. They all stop the imitating after a bit.

Is there anything that would make your job more fulfilling? Easier? More successful? What would you change if you could?

In this centre, I can think of nothing I'd change. We have a bunch of old ECEs and Human Services workers who have been here for a long time without much turnover. They know what to do, and they're always welcoming me in the class. It's always positive. I don't have to tell them a lot of things because they know.

What I want is to go back on the road to go help other centres with inclusion. The centres that have had no inclusion experiences or have only had negative ones. We'll really try to implement that kind of outreach program again. I continue here because I love my kids here and I know them, but I think the need is bigger elsewhere. Here, they can work without me because they did it well before. Now, it would go even smoother because we have more contact with the therapists. That contact is part of what my role as Special Needs Coordinator has brought over the last four years.

When people from the regular centres say, "Gee, we'd love to do integrated child care, but we don't have enough hands," how do you answer that?

We know they can't afford the staff required. Yes, the province does give us a certain amount for each eligible kid (with a special need), but it's not enough to hire somebody. So it's always money. I say just bring one Human Services worker into each child care centre so they can start to include at least a few children. A travelling resource teacher doing the type of work I used to do could assist these Human Services workers in getting started and in learning how to observe behaviour and how to adapt activities.

When I was a travelling resource teacher, I found that some of the child care directors in this province are really good on inclusion. They're really open. So that makes a big difference. They talk about inclusion to their staff, and they promote the attitude, "Wow, that's nice," and, "That's a good challenge."

Unfortunately, I don't think funding resources for integrating child care is a top priority for the government. Their first priority for child care is growth right now. We all know that. And there are a whole lot of pressures to do more and more and more child care, and all the quality things are sort of secondary to that. They never talk about inclusion.

We really want to help other child cares, and we want to give the Ministry a push. We need resources so that teachers and parents can at least get a pre-diagnosis so we know where to go, and we can find the right help and get the child on a list for a real evaluation and appropriate therapy.

Okay, we have the first step, what's next? What happens before the big evaluation? A kid can be in a child care for four years and we will try to deal with his challenges. With some kids' behaviour, it's so hard for the ECEs that some of them just quit, and it's finished. That's why some centres don't want to integrate anymore. They didn't have the help, and they have been crazy for four years with a kid, so it's, "No more. That's it. Finished. Thank you. Bye." I wish we were able to do something to help them, but it's a long process.

We have one kid who came from another child care centre. When he started here, his mother talked about the other centre and how it was so hard to feel that nobody there liked her kid. They thought he had bad behaviour. We told her, "It's Okay. Don't worry. We're going to try. For us, it's so natural. Relax. Don't be scared. It's going to be Okay." She said to call her if we had a problem with the child, and we were able to assure her, "We're not going to call you. Don't worry. Go home." And we have never had to call her because he's so great. Two weeks after he started, she came in and cried, "God, thank you!" We just said, "It's Okay, you know. It's our job. We love to do it."

4

"For Every Child, There is a Place Somewhere"

This centre is another excellent example of an earlier model of inclusion that developed in hospitals and children's rehabilitation centres, and more commonly focused on children with physical and health needs than on children with intellectual disabilities and behavioural disorders. It is licensed for sixty children and enrolls twenty-four with severe special needs. One morning we watched a young, very dapper father bring his severely disabled son to an Early Childhood Educator at this centre. It was clear that the child was welcomed as a real kid. Not to be overemotional about this goodbye moment, but we know that parents often feel that their children with significant disabilities are just tolerated. At this centre, the little boy was really welcomed and valued.

While this centre does not reflect current understanding of natural proportions, like the centre in Chapter 3 it has much to offer to its children and to the broader child care community. Staff such as this can offer essential, tested skills and experience in frontline inclusion practices available nowhere else.

Sharon Hope Irwin: Have you ever had to ask that a child leave your centre?

Centre Director: We accept every child unless we can't give him the resources he needs. If we can't help him, he needs something else.

In 25 years, that has happened twice. Both times, it was with children who were so violent and aggressive that it was hard for the rest of the group to deal with them. Even for someone like me who helps kids, it was hard. They were kids who needed one-to-one, and inclusion, for us, is not one-to-one. Inclusion is working in the whole group.

We weren't a good resource for those kids. We weren't helping them. That's why the director decided that we couldn't keep them. We made the decisions only after doing everything we could, after many consultations. We didn't just say, "We can't help him. Let's put him out." One of those kids stayed here for a year before we decided we could no longer keep him. It's always hard to do that.

Tell me about your staff.

This year, we have three additional staff who support kids in the three classrooms. We have one kid who needs constant attention, and we've made sure that he has that constant attention. Right now, he's not with us. He's at home with his father because he has epilepsy, and they're trying to get his medications adjusted properly.

At the beginning of the year – for us, the beginning of the year is September – we always try to give more support. So we have three staff in the classroom (instead of two) and, sometimes, we have somebody else that comes in from outside and gives us extra help with evaluating needs and suggesting what we can adapt to help the kids. At the beginning of the year, we don't know some of the kids, so we use extra people while we're learning to know them.

Our classroom Early Childhood Educators come from regular training programs. I was an ECE when I came here, and with my basic training and experience I could work well here. What we want first from the ECEs is that they know about kids because all the kids, even the kids with special needs, are kids first. So we don't necessarily look to hire people with additional training or backgrounds in special needs. We look for good ECEs with the right attitude about inclusion. I didn't have a special course to work with those kids. It's the experience. It's having somebody show you how it is done and seeing the way the therapists do it. Now, they're starting to include some issues about inclusion in the regular ECE training program, and we have some people who come here for their practicum.

Also, people involved in this city's child care movement offer different workshops, some on inclusion. That is becoming a popular model of encouraging child care centres to do more inclusion.

We have a person here who does a great deal of consulting with child care staff at the other centres over the phone. "Did you try this? And did you try this? Maybe if you just put a mat under his plate, it won't move around so much, and you won't need somebody sitting beside him all the time when he eats." And, after a month or so, they talk again. "I did try this and it worked, or it didn't work...what else can I do?" Sometimes she calls the parents, too, or the director of the child's centre to discuss ideas to help the child.

When our kids go to school, the therapists and the ECEs meet with people from the School Board, and they decide together which school the child's going to go on to based on their strengths as well as needs. We look for the school that's going to offer the services the child needs. If he goes in a regular school – because sometimes they can go in a regular school with a little support – what do we have to offer him there?

Right now, we have a little child who is in with the babies who needs to be tube fed. We work with that and it's okay. She's so lovely and funny. She's started to walk by herself! There are three ECEs who work there with her so, even if there's one staff who usually takes care of her, the others need to know how to do it, too.

We also have a child with a tracheotomy. She has a hard time breathing, but because our centre is so close to a children's hospital, we feel more secure. We have a phone close, a resource close, and the ECE is not alone in that. There's somebody else with her. A child like her might be harder for a child care centre that is not used to doing that.

Experience is a plus. The ECE our outreach person is going to help is in a position to say, "She knows what she's talking about. She did it before me, and I can have confidence in her."

We have a good structure here, so we're putting together a book with information about the way we work to give tools to other people. It's going to be good! I've read a little bit. It makes people see that they can do it. It's not that hard. The book gives examples of kids and ideas of what you can do to help them.

Describe your vision of inclusion.

We have two committees on the Board. We have one for administration, and we have one to develop our philosophy. The director, ECEs and parents are on both committees. We sit down and we talk about our values, the things we want and the quality we want to give here.

For us, inclusion is best served when you go into the group to work with the kids, to help the ECE, and to do what they are doing. If the group is doing painting and Sheila needs help, we're going to go and help her. She does the same thing as the other kids. We don't take a child out of the group to do something with her. We adapt the activity for the child, so she can play with the others.

For example, when the kids are playing with blocks at the table, Sheila finds it very hard to go and build something with the blocks because her arms are not under her control. So I was playing with her lately and I realized that, for her, the fun was in making the buildings fall down. It would make her laugh. I thought, "Oh that's good! Because she's playing at the same thing. I'm building it for her, but she's playing because she's going like this, and they're falling down, and we're laughing." She's doing the same activity as the other kids in her own way.

Sheila often uses her foot to play. We put Play-Doh on the table, and all the kids play with Play-Doh, and she's playing with it with her foot. One hot, summer day, I was in the room with the kids, and we were putting on sunscreen. I would put two kids together, and they were putting the cream on each other. I was sitting with one kid, and I had Sheila on my lap, and I wanted them to work together. I put Sheila on me so she was closer to the other kid, and she just naturally took her foot and put it in the cream, in the jar, and put it on the arm of the other kid. That is inclusion. She's doing the same thing the way she can do it.

We create Intervention Plans for the children. First, we

take the information from the therapists and from all the people who work around the child, and then we need to adapt our activities so the child can participate. Sometimes we film a child in therapy. Sometimes we have the parents tape the kid at home to see how he works when he eats, or goes to the toilet, or gets ready for bed and then we bring the tape back to the therapist. That information gathering is the starting point. Then we talk about goals and objectives and about the interests of the child, too. What the child likes to do. That's the way we work with them.

We're working, but the child doesn't know that he's working. We call it play. When you're four years old, you learn through play. The therapist would come to get the kid and say, "We're going to go in and work together," and we've told them, "Say 'Play.'"

So the therapists do take the children out for therapy. The therapist has a job to do and that's okay; but, for us, it's different. We go and see the child at his therapy to see what he's working on and what can we adapt. The therapists give us cues when we go to meet with them or when we speak with them on the phone.

Sometimes, the therapists can come and do their therapies in the room with all the kids in the group. Sometimes, too, when a child doesn't want to leave the class, he can bring a friend with him. When the kids are with other kids, the stimulation is always stronger. Sometimes when the therapist sees the child playing, she says, "Oh, with me, he doesn't do that." Well, with us, he does do that because, with the stimulation of seeing his friends do that, he thinks, "Oh, I can do that." So the stimulation of being with the other kids is good.

Have you noticed any trend among the therapists to do more work in the classroom?

Well, it happens but not often. It depends on us. We can ask them, but if they have a block of ten or twelve therapy sessions with a particular child, they're not going to do them all here. They may come here once or twice. I think it sometimes makes sense to do some therapy outside. Like, for language therapy, the therapist sometimes needs to work on something specific that we don't know how to do. For example, the therapist has to do some work with her finger in the child's mouth, but that's something we're not going to do here.

What are you most proud of?

That's a good question for our director because she's very emotional about inclusion and that's how she wants other people to feel, too. It's not only about techniques. It's about children. She's pleased with me because, when I translate the things that she wants to say, I can translate the emotion, too. We're proud that the child care centre here has stayed, and we're proud that now it's starting to spread the news that, for every child, there is a place somewhere.

Our expertise is starting to show more, and we're working directly with the Ministry. The government regulations are that 20% or a maximum of nine children with disabilities can be in the program. We're going to ask the government to keep the 20% and not the maximum of nine, so we can have more kids here.

What are your dreams? If you could make anything happen for this program, what would it be?

I wish I didn't have to have this job anymore. I wish every child had a place in a regular child care centre. That would be good.

My other dream is to make everybody understand that inclusion starts when they're young, when they're small, when they're in a child care for all kids, and it follows them through school, and it follows them when they go to work and on through their whole life cycle.

Our mission is to keep the picture of child care including all kids, a child care for everybody. It's not a centre for kids with special needs here; it's a child care, and we want to keep it that way. We don't want every child to look "normal." He's what he is. One's hair is brown, and the other one is blonde. Each one is different. One is independent. He's going to play with the other kids, but he's also going to go around and pick up something for Sheila, and then he is going to go into the world and he's going to have empathy and understanding naturally.

I didn't see that when I was younger, so it made me more afraid of kids who were different. But my own children came here, so they saw that some people are not independent. And we can talk about that. They're going to see someone outside in the larger world who is different, and it's going to be natural because they saw that before.

If you could go back to when you took this job, 14 years ago, if you could go back to the beginning and make any changes, is there anything you would do differently?

I wish we'd moved more quickly to this collaborative model where we work with everybody involved with the child. Before, everybody worked separately, and now they're working together. It's key for the success of the child. The therapists know that the way we are doing things is good for the child and is stimulating for the child. What they do is good, but what we do is good, too. Everybody involved with the child is important.

5

"I Don't Under- stand Why the System Hasn't Buckled"

Twelve years ago, I watched the director of this child care centre working with a shovel, a trowel, a bag of mix and a hose, pouring concrete from a wheelbarrow. Without missing a sentence of our discussion, she scraped away some sand, turned on the hose, mixed more concrete, and then created a pathway to the combination sandbox-sandtable. My expression asked the question. And in a very matter-of-fact voice she said, "One of our kids uses a wheelchair. I've watched him looking at the sandbox, but the wheelchair can't get through the surrounding sand. So, I thought, it's Friday. I'll build a pathway out of concrete and by Monday it'll be dry."

She was passionate about inclusion and was proud of the many innovations her centre had introduced into the program to make it fully inclusive.

What a change today! In many ways, with that strong commitment to child care, great management skills, and terrific energy, this director is still providing leadership and vision to the field and to the community. But her energies have shifted to issues other than "inclusion" because, as she sees it, government has put up too many barriers. And when I asked her what it would take to bring her program back into the forefront of inclusive child care, it was obvious that her commitment was still there and that with some support, she'd be an inclusion leader again.

Sharon Hope Irwin: Over the past ten to twelve years, how has your centre changed with regards to the inclusion of children with special needs?

Centre Director: We've faced some real challenges as we've expanded, and we've had some real difficulties with the Ministry. Our ability to serve kids with special needs has gone way down as a result.

Back then, at our one site, we had a Special Needs Coordinator and three contract workers to assist children with special needs. The contract workers were hired by us, and trained by us – and became committed to inclusion. In a way, they functioned mainly to reduce ratios, increasing quality while paying particular attention to children with special needs. At every interest area, we posted large index cards that included the names of children with special needs and the goals or objectives that all staff would work on while the children were in that area. This way, both the children with special needs and their support staff were integrated into the entire program of the centre, not segregated within it as so often happens with staff hired to support a child with special needs.

We were told by a Ministry official at a meeting preliminary to our 1995 expansion, "I'm sick and tired of you people doing what you want to do." We were hearing this type of thing instead of being supported and commended for our work because we had been creative with the funding we'd received, and we didn't fit the itinerant resource teacher model they were pushing. Government officials were the ones who did the positive evaluations. They were the ones who did the licensing. They approved all this and then they took it out of our hands.

The itinerant resource support model that they wanted us to implement here involves using an outside agency that provides support and consultation. So, if a child care centre had a child with special needs, that agency would be the first service they would contact. Under that model, you pick up the phone to say, "I have a child with some identified needs," and they would have someone come out and observe.

After coming to observe, they would bring toys and equipment that the child with needs could use and that the other children can use. They would develop the individual program plans when they're on site, and they would ask that the centre's staff complete those plans when possible. "These are the goals. These are the objectives. Work on this." But they would visit only once a month!

The support's not there. It is not hands-on where they teach one of our staff and, in turn, that staff can work with the other staff. There's no real transfer of knowledge. Their services for children with special needs are still really dependent on the child care centres to supply the skills.

They will provide enhanced support for a child who is non-ambulatory and can't feed himself, but it's minimal. Even with the child who we're servicing right now, the agencies that we're involved with recognize the need –

they know that it's desperate – but the reality is the required level of support is not there. This child should really have someone with him at all times when he's with us. I don't believe there's any question of that, but the agencies providing services to our centre for this child's needs are not able to provide us with enhanced support for seven hours a day. The funding is not there.

We get twelve hours a week, and it's up to the director to find the worker for the two-and-one-half hours a day that amounts to. We have to look in the community ourselves to find someone who can work with this child, who can be an extra pair of hands in the room – and who is willing to work two-and-one-half hours a day, and not be paid for days when the child is absent.

That's the model right now. If you have a child with special needs, then you contact the agency. Tantrums. That's all that we get right now.

Ten years ago, we had a number of children with significant needs, and we decided on the curriculum that would best help them. Over where the arts and crafts materials are, and in other areas of the centre, we posted the current activities we were working on and a sentence or two about what we hoped would happen during art time or story time or snack time, etc. That's not defined by us anymore. At that time, the teachers were better funded. Those teachers developed programs for the children in the group care. We don't have those teachers anymore. All that was funding cuts.

So, what we have now, as I described, is an external agency coming in and developing any individual programming that might happen. They come to work on site with the child and develop a plan. Then they present the information to the teachers, indicating what they would like to have happen. But our staff, as such, is greatly limited in what they're able to do. And we don't get the referrals that we used to.

Where are the kids with special needs now? I don't know where those children have gone. There are a lot of children with special needs. These resource teachers from the agencies do go to other child care centres. They carry caseloads, and they service other child care centres. People from government say things like, "Oh, there's no wait list. No, we're able to service everyone that's referred." I'd like to see some documentation to go with that.

When we lost the support funding for children with special needs, we had to realize, "Heads up! We're different now. We don't have the support mechanisms that we used to have." If a child arrives in a wheelchair or with a walker, or is physically challenged, or has behavioural problems, we now have to address up front that we might not be able to accommodate him. How are we going to be able to service that child without extra supports?

We had no track record working with the agencies that were identified to support us. We were used to having a skilled workforce and in-house resource teacher support, and we don't have that now. We just always have to be aware of that.

The agency that provides consultative services and does therapy delivers its services at its own site. They've really stuck to that. They never were itinerant. We tried. We wanted therapy to happen at the child care centre because it made sense to work in the most relaxed environment for the child. It seemed like a natural time to come and see the child—at child care—as opposed to at a one-on-one clinical appointment at the hospital. We tried to get them to come here. It did happen, but only when we clustered kids so they could schedule appointments to see three kids in one morning.

If we provide a service to a group of children, we are committed to providing that service for *all* of those children. We wanted to be an inclusive program, but how inclusive can it be if we're not meeting the needs of the child that has identified needs? How inclusive can it be for the other children in the group if the program is at a lower level because of the additional needs?

Our challenge after losing the funding has been to change the environment, to get extra training. It is almost like we have to start all over again.

I remember talking with you twelve years ago. Back then, the kids with identified needs showed up and, instead of saying, "We can't do it," you were hustling around the city and dragging in resources from everywhere. Now that you're older and wiser and living in a different political climate where things have been torn away from you, why aren't you starting that process again?

I'm cautious. I've stayed in this field because of my love for children, not just children having identified needs. So, you know, there's a responsibility, and there's a level of service that I need to make sure is ongoing for all of the children.

In the past year, we've come close to having to re-evaluate our capacity to keep the child that we're servicing here. Very, very close. His behaviour was escalating, and it was a concern from a safety perspective and when we considered the other children and the staff involved with him. We only get twelve hours of support a week. The other agencies recognize the need. One of the workers with another agency is actually leaving her ECE student who's following her on placement here with us just as an extra set of hands – because there's not enough funding.

I've had to really re-examine whether we should continue to service children with special needs. We were proud of the services that we provided for those children. Now we're seeing whether we can shift the Ministry model again to get supports back beyond once a month consultations. I admit I have not picked up the phone and said, "Why haven't we got referrals?" The Special Needs Coordinator who belonged to our centre staff was one of the funded positions that were pulled. That is part of the reason why we're not picking up the phone looking for children with identified needs because that has become yet another additional responsibility that we take on above and beyond.

I am no longer attempting to say to government, "I want some more information about what you're doing. What are your directions? What are your visions? What are your plans for services for children with special needs? What's the plan?" I now realize that these plans are made long before the attempt to implement them is being made. For me, that's a lesson learned. The Ministry has already determined what's going to happen in child care. It is no longer my role to blacken anybody's eyes or make people feel uncomfortable by questioning their plans.

I'll always have an interest, but the focus isn't on inclusion in the daycare centres; it's on these other agencies. We're not the be-all, fix-all for everyone. We're not servicing a great number of parents that have children with identified needs.

Even parental representation on the Board has changed.

We used to try to help parents of kids with special needs to develop into the most effective advocates they could be for services when their children went to school, knowing that it was a long road. The Family Support Worker in our centre was a key position to assist with that service. So without that link, it doesn't exist.

The provincial government's goals have been to provide fuller parent choice, to have the resources follow the child, and not to spend any more money than they are already spending. So, over a period of time, they closed the specialized nursery schools and they shifted to an itinerant model. They attempted to get agreements with the centres that had integrated licenses that they would give up their resource teachers in return for a menu of services that would be provided through the agencies. Some agreed. Some didn't. We didn't. And eventually they just said, "Well, it's over anyway."

Tell me about how staffing works, or doesn't work, now.

One of the things that I've identified in the history of this centre is that, since 2000-2002, we've had major staff turnover which is different from what you saw ten years ago. So I have spent some quiet time looking at why there has been such a turnover.

Younger staff got married. They moved away. They followed their partners. Low salaries. Low morale, certainly, with what happened to us. They went to work in different fields.

The wage subsidy that we once received is now site-specific. They won't give it to us at our two new sites. We believe that we have the right to manage the money and the right to move the wage subsidy or to allocate it equally amongst staff, but then the City said, "No, you can *only* spend the money here." So that has also affected the services that we are able to provide. We'd like to spread out the senior staff.

Previously, as staff developed skills and ability, we moved them to be anchors at the new sites. Now the City is saying, "If you want those people to get that wage subsidy, they have to work back here." So, they have disrupted the operational goals of the organization. They just continually limit us. All my senior staff with the skills and ability are going to end up back in the city. This is the only site that we have wage subsidies for.

When they pulled the wage subsidy, staff were unable to handle the low wages without that top-up. That's impacted our services for children with special needs. The way the City's dealing with its own resources is inhibiting the growth of child care. There isn't any logic. It's crazy.

We're trying to be more vocal about it with our parents and to get them to be more vocal as well. We have an opportunity this year to move some child care funding that's not being utilized into wage subsidies, and I think we should do it before they decide that they're spending it on something else.

For early childhood educators, nothing's changed. I've been in this position for thirty years, and the salaries are still horrible!

Also, the staffing issue is a huge problem. ECE training has not changed to accommodate children with special needs. The resource teacher training is almost non-existent. You can train someone. You put all that interest into working with children with special needs, and they move on. It's a corridor profession. The resource teachers who are trained are aspiring. They're going out to do agency work. It's just a constant bleed on the child care centres – the constant staffing changes and the fact that the support isn't there.

One of the biggest disadvantages for child care is the parents are with you for only two or three years. Then they're gone and, although they believe in it fervently, they're so busy being parents they can't support the system.

So, because of a variety of factors, we are an example of a program that has had to retrench with respect to its capacity to include kids with disabilities. Our practice can no longer be what it once was.

Does this centre exclude children with any type or level of special need? What limitations do you see your centres as having with respect to difficult-to-serve kids?

Well, initially, there wouldn't be any automatic exclusion. The director would make contact with the parent who identified that their child had special health care needs. There would be a series of questions such as, "Do you have any supports within the home environment right now? What agencies are you connected with? Do they have any home visits set up?" There would be a site visit no different than for any other family. Mom and Dad, Guardian, whomever, comes with the child to visit the centre.

The purpose of the site visit is to seek out how the parent feels about the child joining this group. So, for example, one parent who came to visit in the past – a parent of a physically challenged child – she, herself, said,

"Oh no, we don't want our child in this group. He would get overwhelmed." She didn't want her child in with his appropriate age group, so we accommodated her by putting the child in with a younger age group. I guess the parent wasn't ready for this program. So there may be things like that in the initial visits. It may not be centre-driven.

We allow an opportunity for the parents to express their concerns. It's a balancing act once we establish what the parental needs are and what some of the child's needs are. We network with other agencies, and we give it a shot. Also we try and see if we can accommodate the child. The bottom line would be, "Are we really able to service this child? Are we able to provide an enriched environment for this child? A stimulating environment?"

We also have to consider how our staff who will be working with the child are faring. If they're feeling like they're just not able to be there for the program, and for the other children, we'd look for other support systems. We look for any red flags that seem to say, "Help us!" So far, so good. We've been able to manage that way.

We have a child here who's visibly different. She has dwarfism. Then there are two little boys who have emotional and behavioural issues.

With one boy's family, I don't think they realized or recognized that their child's behaviour was out of the norm until we identified it before he got into school. But, in this particular case, I don't think that the family was fully aware. I think they were just hoping that it would go away. My philosophy is the child is not separate from his family, so we have to make sure some programming is being done at home as well. Otherwise, that's where we become protective of our staff and say, "Look, he can't come here and terrorize our staff with nothing changing at home. It's got to be across the board or it ain't gonna work."

With those boys, an agency did try to come to our rescue. They sort of took us on really quickly because we really needed them. They do psychological testing on children as well as social, emotional, and parenting assessments. The focus is more on the mental health aspects versus developmental ones, although there also may be developmental difficulties. They also would see that speech assessment and any other testing that is needed gets done. They have that at their fingertips.

Still, I have to say that, at this point, I'm not able to give guarantees. I'm not feeling as confident about things as I did years back. Oh, we'd do it! We'd do this and we'd do that. Now, with the changes in supports – we are not funded for any kind of enhanced support – and with finances, the turnover in staff, the subsidy being tied to one place, the low level of early childhood training – all of those things are risk factors. Put them all together, and it spells a real change in what you can do for kids.

What policies guide your three centre sites with respect to the number of children with special needs that they can enroll at any one time?

Again, it's the needs of the group. We look at the group as a whole and what's manageable within the group from the child care perspective as well as from the staff perspective. Are we able to provide an educational program in which all of the children develop? Are the staff able to adapt and manage with the child who is physically challenged? With the child who is academically challenged?

It's wonderful that all sites are now on one floor because

we no longer have to deal with the safety factor of removal. That was certainly an issue of concern at the old site in particular. Children who were non-mobile were on the second floor, and staff had to be constantly adjusted to adapt. Now we're fine. We can just go outside. So that's no longer a restricting factor.

Do you ever modify the hours that a child with special needs can attend?

If the parent is the funder [that is, pays the full fee], the child can be here throughout the day.

If the child is funded by government with a child care subsidy, then we no longer control that. It's controlled by the funding agency. So the City will say, "It's only for relief, so that's only two-and-a-half hours, and not every day." This happened with a child whose Mom had seizures and there were some concerns about delayed development. They wanted the child to spend time in an enriched environment to develop language skills, social skills, and cognitive skills, above and beyond what could be offered at home since the stay-home Mom had health issues and the Dad worked.

This child had attended five days a week, and then the funding structure changed so that, where the placement is for enrichment purposes, the child does not have to be here every day, because the Mom's at home. So the City now has much greater control over who attends these programs if there's a subsidy involved.

Now that child is only funded for two days a week. It was revisited with the funder, but the bottom line is, "That's it." That's all there is. The parents believed so strongly in this that they paid for additional mornings, and I have no idea where they got the money. But they did. The parents found money so their daughter could attend two other times and be here four times per week.

What would it take to restore your capacity to be as pro-actively inclusive as you were a decade ago?

We need some assured hands-on support staff, some definite placements. We need agency funding to be topped up in order for them to truly provide the services that are identified by a centre such as ours. The support that we have from the Itinerant Resource Teacher is at arm's length, and it's once a month. The agencies would be giving us more if they could. We recognize that they're limited.

Also, the agencies should be finding people in the community and giving them some hands-on training to be effective enhanced support workers. The current system creates a lot of administrative work for the centres. Even when the funding is there, it costs our centre money to handle the administration part, which to me is another tax on services to children with special needs.

If you want enhanced support, you have to fill out the application to request the funding. When you're approved, you go find the person. How do you find somebody who's able to provide enhanced support other than looking at your own supply of teachers? You're only going to get twelve hours a week, so you have to determine the schedule that meets your needs. The goal is to spread all of these support systems out so there is good coverage but, at the same time, they are not doubled up on any given day and the classroom environment is not inundated with adults.

Another dream would be to see more enhanced training for Early Childhood Educators. They need a two-year program with particular courses to broaden the teachers' knowledge of children with special needs, but that's not enough.

We need higher salaries for the Early Childhood Educators. There are Early Childhood Educators who are competently managing children with special needs in a group setting with enhanced support or support from other agencies. Staff who have the skills and ability to provide programming for children with special needs with enhanced support need to be recognized financially for their work. It's embarrassing what Early Childhood Educators make.

When I first started as Executive Director, someone on the Board was very nervous with the fact that I had gotten this job because I had spoken out in a news article calling for higher salaries for Early Childhood Educators. He was very anxious about that and, in a private finance meeting, he said, "You know we don't have that kind of money. You know what we're paid. Why would you make those statements?" I still believe in the importance of paying Early Childhood Educators decently. Better pay leads to a higher level of professionalism.

I don't understand why the system hasn't buckled. If we don't address that system, the whole early child care world is going to fall apart. If we don't have the workers in child care, there won't be any child care, let alone services for children with special needs. All this has to be grasped by the powers that be – and quick!

In order to be more inclusive, we need people to act as designated case managers for kids with special needs. With different agencies providing pieces of support, no one takes the lead role. Our centre has become the case coordinator in some respects, although that's not officially in anyone's job description. We all just talk on the phone and get ourselves organized. That is typical, "Whoops, there's nobody here to do it." So we've just created something to make it work, to deal with it.

The worker who comes to be with one of our kids with special needs indicated there's going to be a meeting next week for all of the agencies that are involved. We're going to be at the table, and the parents are going to be there. The parents are really key in all of this, too. Regular meetings like that for child care children don't exist anymore. Now, we just do that above and beyond to make it work on a totally volunteer basis.

Case management is another uncompensated task for our centre. The case management or case coordination for our special needs children often becomes our responsibility. A logical progression would be, if the child comes in unidentified, the teacher would approach the lead teacher and say, "We're having a problem with Johnny at snack time," or whatever. The lead teacher is a senior staff person with more experience. She may be a little more intuitive as to what's going on in the group and could make some suggestions. Were it not resolved at that level, then they would bring it to the director's attention.

What's happened lately is that it has gone directly from front-line staff to the director, with the teacher saying, "This child has become a problem." Couple that with new staff, inexperienced staff.... Help! Case coordination has fallen by the wayside, and we're picking up the pieces – taking up our time with no additional funding.

How do the parents receive their information about what's happening?

We like the idea that the parents get information directly from the ECE first. In some circumstances, the director might provide information to parents. That's pretty well it. In regard to children with special needs, the other agencies direct the parents to the child care centre.

Tell me how your Board of Directors views inclusion.

I don't think the present Board is knowledgeable about services that we provide or knows that we're trying to have an inclusive program. We don't receive funding to provide those services anymore, so it's not something that would be obvious for the Board to consider.

Does the centre have a formal policy on inclusion?

I knew you were going to ask me that. There is no written policy. Basically, the programming that we provide meets the needs of all children in all levels of development, but it doesn't speak specifically to the special needs population or culture.

Before, we could say, "If we can do it, we'll do it." We are not that strong anymore. Sad. Now, often, we can't do it. If we do it, we're providing ammunition for the government to say that theirs is a successful way of doing things, which is not the message we want to send because, realistically, we need more. It would strain our capacity in many ways to provide services to kids with needs, by pulling out of our resources rather than government's.

Can you tell me about how transitioning to school works?

We have two sites that are hooked up to the school, and it's a benefit, because people from the school will come to those sites. We've had the principal actually come down and get feedback from us when they know that the child's leaving us and going into the school system. That's when they come down the hall real quick! They're suddenly our best friend. So we do give them a lot of information about what we have learned about the child. Often, the agency people who have worked here with us, if there is somebody from an agency, will give the school some feedback as well.

Back when we had our own Special Needs Coordinator, she would go into the school, make sure everything went smoothly, and make sure all the information was transferred. It was just perfect. OK, so now who's going to do that? It just won't exist. It is now up to the parent to decide if they want to tell the teacher about their child's difficulties.

We take on the unofficial role of case manager for some of the children with special needs in order to be coordinating at the school in conjunction with the parents. In this particular situation we're dealing with right now, the child would be kicked out of kindergarten on the second day of school if we didn't help set things up for him. That's what the person from one of the agencies actually said to me when she was doing an observation. She said that, if this continues to occur when he's in the kindergarten, from what she has seen, they wouldn't have him in the school system. It's discretionary. Until the age of six, they can refuse them. He'd be back with us, I'm sure, and I don't know if we could take him back.

Technically, we don't have case managers to transition the kids into the schools, but we have identified staff who do some of that voluntarily. Someone on our staff would say to the parent, "What are your plans for September?" On the other hand, we have some children who are being seen by people from the agencies, and we really don't have a direct contact with their future schools.

How do you take these things to the Board?

The Board would not perceive these as issues that I would need to bring back to them. The governing Board sets me with the responsibility to work with staff and to review and revise the job descriptions.

This new building provides a wonderful new environment....

Working in our old environment helped us create this new environment. We've had life spans in this early childhood field that some people are never going to see. Now we've merely gone off and defined spaces and created environments and hired the staff to make it all work. We're still underpaid and undervalued but, my God, you have got to look at the stuff that's good. It's been stressful times, but we've also had some really good times together because we can work it out and see some successes and have some laughs.

What is your wish list for this centre, regarding inclusion of children with special needs?

We need support in five major areas:

1) Most important is higher salaries for frontline ECE staff, or you won't have a system to fix. I get very nervous when I hear "expansion; expansion" with no attention to supporting staff. There is high turnover in child care now, with very quick exiting of our best ECEs into better-paying work in other agencies such as Early Years Centres, family resource centres, family support programs, and so forth. Most of our staff are young and minimally trained, putting increased pressure on our senior staff to train and support them. The system has to be shored up before it is expanded.

2) In addition to across-the-board salary increases, there needs to be some kind of system to recognize staff skills and abilities beyond the basics.

3) We desperately need on-going professional development for staff working in centres with children with special needs. This training must also be incorporated into basic ECE training.

4) We need much more additional staffing when we enroll children with special needs, either organized through us or through an agency. "Enhanced support workers" who are hired through an agency need a lot of support to do their job in our centres, and it's an invisible tax on my staff to do that job over and over again. I can accept this, but there is a need to recognize how much we have to do to make an agency system work. The fundamental problem here has been the critical under-funding of the agency's budget for enhanced support workers.

5) We need a Special Needs Coordinator again, who would be the link between the family, other services and agencies, and direct connection with my staff. She would also be the case coordinator, meeting with families, identifying skills and strengths, planning, developing IPPs, meeting with therapists, modeling techniques and strategies for the system, and coordinating with schools for the transition from child care.

But most important, before I leave the system, I'd say "Fix the salaries." Many of the other issues would be less critical if the base – the frontline child care staff – were well compensated, had strong training, had high morale, and could treat child care as a real career.

6

"Thank God, They Were the Baby Teeth"

When we visited this centre twelve years ago, the director was a passionate inclusion advocate. Their enrollment included children with significant disabilities, and they actively promoted inclusion within the community. Today, along with typically developing children, they only accept children with mild disabilities.

The new director had been on staff for twenty-one years when she took over the position five years ago, but she now feels that with constant staff turnover and the severe limitations of the government support for children with special needs, it is impossible to properly provide for children with significant special needs.

Sharon Hope Irwin: Over the past ten to twelve years, how has your centre changed with regards to the inclusion of children with special needs?

Centre Director: Well, I've been the director for five years now, but I was on staff at this centre for 21 years, so that means I've been around for 26 years total.

There have not been a lot of big changes over the last ten years or so, but some things are different. In the past few years, we have had children with milder disabilities. When we started the integrated program, the children with needs had greater disabilities. We worked with quite a few families whose children were handicapped, or were in wheelchairs, children with spina bifida, that type of disability. We are able to accommodate children with greater needs because we are wheelchair accessible, but now we are seeing more developmental delay and language and behavioural problems. A lot of children come in who have not been identified.

I think one of the reasons we're enrolling children with milder disabilities – children whose needs have not been diagnosed – is that the families don't want to identify it because they're afraid they might not get a space if they are identified. So once they start at the child care centre, we of course identify these children. Therefore, we very rarely have room to bring in a child from the City's special needs waiting list – children who have been identified with more severe disabilities. It's always been a struggle for families of children with special needs to find inclusive centres, so that is one of the reasons why they hide it. I know four families on the City's waiting list whose children have identified needs that have been waiting for the last year.

When I attend meetings with the City and with other agencies, they always talk about the City's central waiting list of children with special needs. Because the five special needs spaces are always filled from the inside, we never have the opportunity to go to the central waiting list. We have not had spaces. A lot of our children are not labeled as high needs only because they're not in wheelchairs, but they do have disabilities, whether it's behavioural problems or language delays.

We're actually licensed to take five kids that have some kind of diagnosed disability, but we always have more than five. Right now, my Special Needs Coordinator is working with *ten* children with very low disabilities and has been in consultations regarding a couple of other children.

It is very difficult to get an extra person for the classroom unless you have children who have very high needs, are in wheelchairs, etc. The City manages that money, and they will pay a person for forty hours to come in and help that child integrate into your program. It cannot exceed forty hours total. It depends on how you want to use this person's time. You can use that person full time for one week, and that's your forty hours; or you can use them a couple hours per day over a longer period. In the past, we had a child here who needed to be fed, so we used that extra person at lunch time. After the five weeks, the staff had to cope at lunch time, and it wasn't easy.

We are fortunate to have students here to help all the time, but they're just sort of getting in and feeling the field.

What are some of the challenges you have faced in maintaining an integrated program?

Being director is a very isolating job. There are a lot of ups and downs. You're on your own. It's not like you work in the classroom where you share your pains with your partner. I don't share my pains with my staff, but I do share them with my Board. Sometimes they sympathize with me. Other times, I don't even want to go and tell them my pains because they're paying me for doing this job. So, you know, you're pretty well on your own.

Before all these cutbacks, child care directors had a sort of support network. We had consultants who would help us deal with issues when it came to the building facilities or dealing with school principals and staff in the school, and making sure that our children got into the kindergarten program. Now, with all those cutbacks, they have just one consultant in the whole city. So this person has to go to all the meetings with the City because we *don't* attend those meetings.

Then the consultant gets all these phone calls from all the directors saying, "Look, I need one washroom to be painted. I put a work order in six months ago, and they didn't even get back to me. The government is saying I'm not going to get licensed if this washroom doesn't get painted...." So those are the issues she also has to deal with. And the consultant doesn't deal with staffing issues. You have to solve those issues in the centre.

In terms of general staff turnover, there have been quite a few changes over the last four years. We had maternity leaves. We had a few staff who decided that they had done enough in this field, and they moved on to go to university. Salaries are always one of the reasons for people to move on. Then a few people also changed fields.

One of the biggest struggles that I have encountered during my five years in the office is hiring a Special Needs Coordinator who will stay. It's been hard for me to keep staff for more than two years. They graduate, they come in, they have experience, and then they move on to consulting or to working in the bigger agencies for more money.

So that's been a concern for my Board and for myself. In five years, I have probably had about eight or nine Special Needs Coordinators.

It has been that way because of funding and because of

lack of training opportunities. The salaries are not compelling. By going and doing consulting or working for a bigger agency, the salary you make is higher. People also think the challenge is greater. People get experience and then they want a challenge. As for the training, the college has one course. It's part of the ECE Program. It's called Special Needs, and that gives them a little bit of preparation. Sometimes they also do placements at our centre with our Special Needs Coordinator. We didn't have a student this year, but in the past we had quite a few students who came in and just shadowed the Special Needs Coordinator during their placements. Centres that have inclusive programs also offer workshops.

The City is definitely not going to give us any more money for a Special Needs Coordinator. We already tried that. The child care centre is already putting money from our budget into the salary because we only get about $30,000 from the city and our Special Needs Coordinator makes $36,000. We're already subsidizing her salary, and we also fund the benefits.

Every time I hire, I ask people if their intentions are to stay at least two years. I was fortunate enough to have a Special Needs Coordinator last year who stayed two years but, after her, I'm already on my second one. I had one that stayed for six months and then she left. Now we have a new Special Needs Coordinator who is a wonderful person.

It's a big challenge for the Special Needs Coordinator because we have four classrooms. She has to go from room to room and work with six or eight different Early Childhood Educators. It's not her classroom. She just goes in and works with those children. She has to get along with everyone and get to know all those different personalities and not take sides and share the classroom.

Do you get visits from Occupational Therapists, Physical Therapists, and Speech and Language Pathologists?

Yes, we do and I think this city is very fortunate. We have a lot of services out there for the children. We have been able to connect with consultants to come in and meet with our Special Needs Coordinator.

There is a waiting list, there's no doubt about it – especially for Speech Services – there is a waiting list of six months, but eventually those children get in.

Sometimes the consultants might come in and visit one child in a classroom, and they might say, "Look, I noticed this. This is what you can do." Even though this child is still on a waiting list, they might say to you, "Look, yeah, I notice so-and-so is having a hard time and stuttering, he's on a waiting list...but for the time being while he's waiting, maybe you can try this."

They also offer a program called "Learning Language and Loving It,"* and I'd say about a half of my staff benefited from that program. Now I have new staff, and we might do it again.

We are very fortunate here. We have three Professional Development days every year, and there are always a lot of workshops that are free for the staff to attend after hours. It's paid time.

Also, each staff gets $200 for Professional Development time a year. So if they attend a couple of workshops that we need to pay for, and if some people don't use their

* Weitzman, E. (1992). *Learning language and loving it: A guide to promoting children's social and language development in early childhood settings.* Toronto: Hanen Centre.

Professional Development money, I'm usually flexible and let the other people attend a workshop that might cost more than the $200.

What aspect of your program are you most proud of?

Definitely it is carrying on the Special Needs Program. Having the Inclusion Program has been great, and I feel proud that I was able to carry that. There have been a few times when I kind of felt, "OK. Are we going to continue this program? Are we going to find somebody to fill that position?" It's definitely been a challenge. I didn't have a Resource Teacher for a period of about four months last year and for a couple of months this year. Those children were still attending the program, and most come by bus, so I had to be the person running back and forth, making sure that I go to my meetings, and that I'm here at 11:30 to take them back to the bus.

The families that we serve are very supportive. There's a lot of parent involvement, so that's a plus for our centre. Our parents are very much aware of everything that is happening. I have twelve Board members, and I usually have about twenty parents at my Board meetings on a monthly basis. Parents like to know what's happening in the program, what's going on, where they can help, and why the children don't have enough toys outside, and so on. They come to the Board meetings and they ask those questions.

So our parents do pay attention to the whole picture of the child care, the program, and staffing, who's there, who's not there, why we don't have enough qualified staff. They're very much aware.

Just to give you an example of the level of parent involvement, I'll tell you about what went on during March Break. We don't let our children watch television or movies except as a special treat. I was short-staffed during March Break, so we put on what we call a learning movie for the children. The next day, I had a few phone calls. Parents were asking me, "Is this part of your program? Are you going to continue letting the children watch TV? Because we don't agree." I had to explain, "No, this was just a special thing for March Break."

One of the things that I feel proud and happy about is the fact that a lot of the families come back. I have children of children attending the centre now. Quite a few children come back, and they're now in university. It's nice to see those people. It's a very rewarding aspect of this job. They give referrals and they talk about the centre and how much their children enjoyed being here. I have families that come and say, "I heard a lot of good things about your centre."

Working with children is always rewarding. Coming in and seeing the smiles. Going into the classrooms and getting hugs.

What guides you in deciding whether you can take a child or not?

In situations where the child's needs have been identified, we have the family come and visit the centre with the child. A consultant usually does the referral. She brings the child in with their family. They meet with our Resource Teacher. They ask her questions, and then they visit the classroom. Then we have team meetings with our Resource Teacher and with the staff in the classroom.

Extra support for integration is, as I said, a person coming in a few extra hours but, after that, you're on your own. So making it work often takes a lot of meetings and a lot of consultations.

We try to predict how including the child will affect the program. I worked with a toddler in the Toddler Room, I'd say probably about seven years ago, and this toddler was always crying during sleep time. We had nine toddlers that needed to sleep and one child who cried for three months non-stop. There were days that you went home and you just felt like crying because you were too tired or it was too difficult a day.

But, you know, we try our best. That's all we can do.

How do you frame what seems to you an appropriate proportion of kids with disabilities?

We have a lot of kids with mild disabilities. We would like to add a couple of high needs children who have been waiting for a while because, even though our staff might think that our children are high needs, I tell them that these children are not high needs. I go to centres that have four, five, even six children with behavioural problems, and they don't have a Resource Teacher. I tell them we're blessed that we have an extra person that we can call if someone has a bad day, or a hard day.

So I think our centre can do more, and that's one of the reasons why I would like to bring at least two more children with greater needs in this summer.

Our children are mostly full-time. We do have a couple of part-timers, but they're only part-time because the families chose to be part-time. We're fortunate enough to have a Resource Teacher on site, so we don't really have to ask families to bring children for part-time if we have the full-time space.

I find, in the past few years, a lot of the doctors prescribe child care for some children with language problems. They recommend that children whose mothers are home attend child care part-time. The children need to be in programs with other children to aid their language development. So often those are the families that need part-time because Mom is at home. She's not working. She only needs part-time, and she can only afford part-time. We have children who attend kindergarten in the morning and come to our centre in the afternoon, so I bring the part-time children in for the mornings. A lot of them are children who have English as a second language.

There is the odd time that a child with special needs is here with us but is not fully participating. There's no doubt about it. Even though we have our Resource Teacher, we have four classrooms, and if we have children who need extra help in different rooms, it is very difficult for her to be in all the rooms. I've been at centres where a child is in a corner playing by herself or not even playing, just sitting there. We try not to have that happen.

I knew of a preschool child who was on the central special needs waiting list at a time when we had twelve children with mild disabilities. The consultant came in and she said, "This is a perfect place for this child because the child would be in a wheelchair and could go outside and crawl around." But it really takes an extra person to make that work. Otherwise, I imagined this child outside and it touched my heart just to think of her crawling on the concrete or just sitting in her wheelchair. I thought to myself, "That's going to be very hard in the wintertime." Staff have shifts and there are times during the day that you only have one staff. I mean, yes, we would manage. Yes, we could cope. But, without the Resource Teacher, certain times during the day would be very difficult.

I had a phone call from a mom last week. Apparently someone told her that we're an integrated centre, and she looked us up, and she called me. Her child is already seven. I gave her information for all the agencies and for the city so we'll see if she can connect with somebody to get a space for her child. She did say to me that she has been on a waiting list all these years since the child was born, and she has never been able to access a program.

My heart goes out to those families. Hopefully somebody will be able to help them.

Do you play any particular role in encouraging the parent participation of these kids with disabilities? Anything you don't do with your other families?

No. I pretty well treat them the same. They're invited to be on the Board, to attend all the meetings, and so on.

One of the things that I often do is talk to the other families and educate the other families about our kids with special needs and why some of them are aggressive. They were fortunate enough to have a child that doesn't need the extra support, but this particular child in this program needs extra support, and they have to be understanding that we are trying to provide a service.

We have a child now who has been with us for three years and there have been ups and downs as far as his physical aggression. I have had parents come here to say, "I've talked to you already, I'm going to withdraw my child if you don't do anything about it." I have to go back, and meet with the staff to talk about putting more things in place to help this particular child. When are the problems happening? Is it during transition? Is it during outdoor time? When should we work one-on-one with him?

Sometimes staff asks me, "Why are you trying to accommodate all this? Why can't you tell this family that we can't just service the needs of this child." I've never done that. In the past, when we had children with high needs, parents wrote letters to my Board and so on. One of the things that I always do is advocate for that particular family because we're an integrated centre. I feel that, because we have this program, we owe back to the families. So there have been times where both my Resource Teacher and my parents felt that we needed to let a child go, but it has never happened. We always managed to keep the child until the end.

A couple of years ago a child pushed another child in the playground and the child lost his two front teeth. Thank God they were the baby teeth. It was not permanent, but this family sued the child care centre. I had to have my Resource Teacher do one-on-one with this child from 12:30 until 5:30 or 6:00 every day.

Our insurance took over. They settled with the family. But it was hard, because the family ended up withdrawing their child, and it was actually one of the parents on my Board, so that was very hard because, when you have issues like that, at Board meetings you do nothing but talk about those issues.

Those times where parents would walk in my office and say, "If that happens one more time, you're gonna hear from me." I'd go outside and tell the staff, "Look, Guys, you need to position yourself here," and I'd talk to the Resource Teacher and I'd say, "Look, you need to do this…." It's hard, you know. It's not easy. But we manage. We cope. And we're still blessed that we have our Resource Teacher….

7

"For a While, She Ate Dirt"

From the beginning, this child care centre included children with special needs. By at least 1992, it had a zero-reject policy which it has maintained to this day. It has recently added an after-school program because, as the director says, the school children with special needs had nowhere to go after school, in the summers, and on school holidays. We should note that this centre has had the same director since its inception, and this may offer a clue to the continued vitality of its inclusion vision. This centre also enrolls children with more and more complicated needs, such as severe eating disorders. Almost all therapies are delivered right at the centre, through a provincial outreach system that gives specific plans and exercises that fit into their routines and programs.

Sharon Hope Irwin: How has your centre changed with regards to inclusion of children with special needs during the last ten or twelve years?

Centre Director: We added a child care program for school-aged children. We did this mainly because there wasn't an acceptable place for our school-aged children with special needs to go. We had several kids here as preschoolers —one was in a wheelchair so had to have a building that was accessible, a couple of them had behaviour problems—and when it came time to find a school-age spot for them, there was nobody who was willing to take them, so we did.

Kids couldn't get placement. That's the way it started. At first we only included two or three kindergarteners with special needs who were fairly easy to include with our preschoolers, but when we wanted to add children up to age 12, we had to make more provisions. We certainly didn't want to segregate these children, so we added a school-aged program for typical children as well as for children with special needs. Other than our integrated program, there is only a specialized after-school program for children with special needs in our area.

Our centre has also changed in some rather subtle ways. One is that more issues are being recognized as potentially disabling. For instance, we started a feeding program. We have several children now who have been seen by various professionals in an eating clinic for preschoolers. These children were off the bottom of the growth charts. They were at the point where they would have been hospitalized and fed intravenously because they were not taking in enough nutrition. That type of malnutrition is linked to brain damage and other problems. These kids may not even make it. One of the things they're doing is trying to track and see if this is a precursor of some kind to anorexia or bulimia.

We're more aware of autism and Asperger's and things like that. It used to be that, if a child was functioning cognitively in a pretty positive way, there was a tendency not to worry. The other social and communication and gross motor skills would come along, so people thought. Now the clumsiness and those things are being more clearly recognized as part and parcel of larger issues. So we've had much more solid intervention with Occupational Therapy, Physical Therapy and Speech. Before, some targeted children were getting Occupational Therapy or Physical Therapy on a weekly basis, but other children didn't get any. Now, there are still a few children who are getting it on a weekly basis, but there's also much more consultation with therapists about all of the children perceived to have needs, and the therapists come right into the centre.

Therapists are now part of a provincial outreach system. Once a month, they give us specific things to do, specific plans, specific exercises, and they'll come back again in a month. That's been quite good, because that's caught up a lot of the kids that didn't get on the list before because they weren't drastic. But you knew. You watched the child who couldn't stand up, reach for the sky, and touch her toes. For the kids whose hamstrings are so tight they can't touch their toes, it means that they can't sit cross-legged for a story, so they get uncomfortable and you get, not serious acting out, but you get some of that discomfort interfering when you've got cognitive stuff going.

It is a better use of therapeutic time to do it this way. Sure it puts a lot more resource burden on our staff, but my staff end up feeling better about what they're doing because they feel like they're approaching the problem with some back-up and some recognition of their competence.

People keep saying to us that we still are quite unique. Well, we don't expect that we're always going to know what to do next, but we do recognize that there are things that we can do. We go back to the experts when we need to. This arrangement is enabling for the staff and empowers them to meet the demands that are really there.

So the kids do most of their therapeutic programs in the child care centre. They may still have a program for extreme hearing loss elsewhere but, if they do, that's the only one that they have outside.

We really have not had too much trouble. You know, we have been able to get informed professionals on the phone if we can't get them to come in. I wouldn't guarantee you that everybody says the same thing, but we really have not had trouble getting the help we need. We get good cooperation because the therapists know that we will actually carry these things out.

Another change is that we see more children with more complicated needs – autism, tube feeding. In the summer, we have one little boy on a stretcher who is here because his family needs child care. As our Resource Teacher once said, when asked about limits, "If they breathe, they are in." We're willing to have an externally-funded support worker support a child with Autism who attends part-time and receives ABA training at home. When the ABA program was unable to hire enough support staff and were sending in three different people each week, we allowed the mother to be the ABA-support worker here.

Another positive change is that we now have three-month reviews. It hasn't happened universally, but it has happened in this centre. The Provincial Coordinator is usually here on the three-month reviews. I think that the reviews keep everybody in line. I know that lots of times you get ready for a review – we don't necessarily do a formal report every three months, not a formal written report – but we get together with the parents and say, "This is what's been happening. What happens in the home…?" So that way we touch base and we are ready to go on to the next piece. By having that three-month kind of thing, and people knowing that it is there, you kind of keep working in a more focused way. Otherwise, it is easy to say, "Well, tomorrow…"

Is there pressure to provide a very different curriculum for the kids with autism?

No. Because I wouldn't agree to doing that. They tried to do that before, and I just said, "No, if that's the way it has to go, then you're going to have to find another place because I think children need time to be children." I can't see sitting down with somebody for eight or ten hours a day, and doing behavioural modification because that approach doesn't relate well to this setting. The child learns a piece, but learns it in a different setting, and then is expected somehow to magically generalize. I don't think that's a very effective learning method. You're stopping the social interaction!

I could just spit sometimes. I had a child in tears yesterday because his mother wanted him to stay for lunch – which he used to do fairly regularly – but, I think, because he started the ABA program – he has now refused to come to the table for activities. I think he's refusing to come for activities because it is yet another time that he has to sit down and do something and produce. I think he's starting to be so fearful of that, or so resistant to it, that he doesn't end up getting the pleasure that he used to get out of making something. In the meantime, this little gal from the ABA program sits here with her notebook and counts up how many times he spoke to somebody. Anyway….

I know that our approach has helped a lot of autistic kids. When Mary, one of our autistic kids, walks in and talks to me about school, I think, "Dr. Smith said she'd never have meaningful language." She certainly has problems, but she's an amazing success.

This year Mary had a new TA. Her name is Mrs. Grant. There's another autistic child in her class who had Mrs. Grant last year, and he wanted to have her again. He didn't get her this time, so he told Mary that Mrs. Grant was a witch, and she was evil. Well, Mrs. Grant came to the first session and Mary was under the table screaming, "You're a witch! You're evil! Get out of my face!" So she still has her unrealistic reactions but, at the same time, it was at the extreme end of a normal reaction.

I received a little note from Mrs. Grant saying that there was a problem. Mary and I sat and talked about how witches aren't real. I could say to her, "That boy was teasing you because he wanted to have Mrs. Grant again. He knew how good she was." Well, you know, it immediately changed, and she has a wonderful relationship with Mrs. Grant.

Mary does have her moments. She flew off once and came in the door yelling, "I wanna get naked!" She literally stripped down to her underwear. It was because she had spilled something on her shirt at lunch, and they had given her a shirt to wear that wasn't hers. She wanted that shirt off. Finally, I said to her, "This shirt's a little bit scratchy. Would you like a different one?" Well, immediately the temper tantrum ended. "Can I have a different one?"

She's quite a gem. She's actually doing quite well in school. For a while, she ate dirt. She had specific sidewalk cracks that she went to, and she scooped up the dirt and ate it. So we went from dirt to brown sugar and a few other things to get her off the dirt.

Certainly it costs more to educate her than it does an average child, but think of what it would have cost to put her in a group home for all of her life. She's going to be a functional adult. She may have difficulty – although she's doing pretty well with math now – but she may have some difficulties and need some kind of social support for a few things. But she may not. She may find it in other ways, because she's really become quite a nice kid and has enough other interests in music and art and stuff like that that she may find a few kindred souls that can tolerate her eccentricities and help her through. I think we helped her access a different future, a *very* different future, than the one she was headed for.

Someday in the distant future, you might consider going to a different job, or retiring. How do you expect the inclusion quality of your child care centre to be maintained after you leave?

I know that, in order to maintain inclusion, we would need a person with effective, efficient writing skills – the kind of person who can write, "Let me tell you about this child," and really warm a bureaucrat or politician's heart.

While I hate sounding elitist, I have to say that fewer high quality students are going into Early Childhood Education. Low wages and minimal career prospects discourage many potential ECEs, and it also seems that government is targeting already marginalized people to become ECEs.

I'm spending more and more time helping staff understand the "why" as well as the "what." For example, we sing "ba, ba, ba, ba" instead of certain words in one of our songs. That's not just because it is fun; it is also because one of the children is working on "ba, ba, ba" sounds, and we can incorporate them into our song. I hope that more knowing "why" will help all our staff keep the practice of inclusion as well as the philosophical commitment.

We have some staff who will stay on here a little longer than I will who will certainly keep things going for a while. But, you know, the directors are the ones who set the stage. And, if that's really the case, then it leaves me a little fearful, because there's no two ways about the fact that with inclusion you have to work a little harder at it to do it right. You get some great gratification from it, but you have to work very hard.

In hiring, I'm looking for people who demonstrate a commitment to inclusion. Everybody knows what we want and can give the politically correct answer, but people who really understand what the job entails are the ones we want. The three-month probationary period often weeds out the staff that don't fit, and sometimes we have to extend the probationary period if we aren't sure.

Some centres that were once inclusive have fallen back. We've been doing it for longer, so that hopefully helps to keep that from happening. We've never done Affirmative Action, per se, for children with disabilities in Canada, but our policy has some of the same reasoning behind it. I think that the more you have in place, the more you make that an expectation. When you make it an expectation, then it starts happening. If you don't have it in place, it doesn't happen, as it didn't for many years. It was the daycare office saying that there would be support for including children with disabilities that made it start happening in most centres.

I guess it can become the same thing as Affirmative Action, and you can get the same kind of backlash that you get from Affirmative Action. You could get parents saying, "Why does that child get more support than my child does? My child's just as important." You could have that kind of stuff happening. We haven't seen too much of that, but I certainly recognize that it could be out there without any trouble and that's why we say to parents, from the beginning, "You will see more children with disabilities here," and so on and so forth. We try to explain that we are enhancing the ratios for everyone.

What is the role of your Board in promoting inclusion?

We recruit our Board carefully. They are incredibly supportive. Some of them see children with special needs as an important part of their typically developing children's early education. The children learn about differences, empathy, finding different ways to do things, problem solving and the like.

Our Board is comprised of people who are committed to the idea of inclusion. People have come to this centre for multiple reasons, but one of them is that their children have learned the value of accepting other people at the centre. They feel that, in being here, their children have learned something more about social values.

We have people who are socially committed to seeing inclusion happen in a decent program. As long as we can keep the program at a reasonable level, then they like what happens to their kids. Their kids are more compassionate. They're less afraid of other people because they've seen that people can just be. So it is not as frightening.

When you look at your successes, what do you say are the major things you have made happen in terms of inclusiveness in your centre?

I would say creating tolerance, but it is more than tolerance; it is real acceptance.

You know, one of the people who worked here many years

ago – she has since retired – is quite overweight. She had done some subbing at another centre, and one of the things that she said to me once was, "Nobody asks me why I'm fat at this centre. The kids don't say, 'Boy, are you fat!'" Whereas, when she went to other centres, that would be one of the first responses she got. Now, it was over with quickly, as soon as the child had said it. She was not making a derogatory statement about those other children. What she was saying is the children here see so many people – because we've also tried to be multicultural – and people in every size and shape and colour, they end up seeing the value of each one, and they don't necessarily think they need to comment on what would be seen as a negative elsewhere.

I am missing some bones in my neck, and kids here will sometimes ask me why I don't have a neck. More often it is, "Why is your chin down there on your tummy?" But, nobody dwells on it. You know, they ask one time, and they're given an explanation. I explained that I am missing bones in my neck to one little girl who had just two fingers, and she smiled and kissed me and said, "Then we're twins. I'm missing bones in my hand, and you're missing bones in your neck!" If a child has a disability, our staff has been so careful about explaining to kids what is going on with the child and why they can't do this or can do something else. It just brings about acceptance.

We had a parent who said her child had been afraid the first day that she came here when she saw Emily, a Black staff member. They had come from the country and there just weren't any Black people there! This child had been frightened at first, but it was, like, a week later that the mother came in and said, "The first one she goes to is Emily!" It was very neat.

I have a student from the university here who comes

from a family with a lot of illness and disability. Her mother died of lupus when she was eight. She has a brother who has pretty extreme autism. He was five when their mother died, and her younger sister wasn't quite two. The father remarried, reversed his vasectomy, and had two more children, one of whom is autistic, and the other one has juvenile diabetes. So this eighteen-year-old has these siblings, only one of whom, the sister, is "normal." She lives in the country and sometimes has had to help out at the local child care because they wouldn't keep her brother if she wasn't there.

So, when this student came here, we had this little guy in a wheelchair with a feeding tube, and the kids were coming over to play with him. He hit a thing with a ball and they would go and catch the ball. She said, "I can't even believe it. At the child care where my brothers were, they would have just pointed and laughed at him."

Our typically developing kids know that they can have an enjoyable interaction with this kid. You know, it takes some setting up, but it gives them a chance to run around and do something that they like to do. "Oooh, okay, can you do it again?" And they get into it because we get into it. There's modelling that's going on. They like to be with the people that are with the child with special needs. There is no staring and pointing a finger and laughing. It is a very different kind of reaction to difference.

I think parents have learned from their kids, too. The parents, I think, were almost parroting what they knew was the politically correct line of thinking, but when their children acted on it, then they really saw it in a different framework. The parents wouldn't have had the same experiences growing up because kids with special needs were not part of their growing up. It is one thing to read about those things, and it is another thing to watch your child live them. So I think that we have made a more general kind of impact.

Our vision of inclusiveness gets shared and passed along in various ways. I was at a wedding on the weekend of one of the kids who had been here when she was three. She is now almost thirty. So 27 years ago, when I first started, she was here. Now, 27 years ago we didn't have very many children with special needs. She is a teacher now. She was going to be a teacher from the time that she was here. From the time she was four, she had decided that she wouldn't let her mother throw away any of her things because she was going to use them when she taught. She was a really funny kid. Now she's teaching other people about inclusion and acceptance.

What are your biggest challenges in maintaining and promoting inclusion?

Funding's certainly always huge.

We have a unique arrangement with the province where block funding for our special needs program is based on average expenditures three years in a row. But, even with the block funding, we note every hour that we spend on extra staffing, including time off the floor to meet with parents or service providers. The block funding doesn't recognize Director's time either. It only recognizes time on the floor.

There is a lot of pressure on us to take more kids with special needs, to combine several high needs children under support from one special needs worker, or to just take them. We gave in last year and had to pay for more assistance out of our regular budget. We can't do that. Some kids simply need one-to-one support all of the time. Some, like those with FAS, need it often but unpredictably. We can't say which day will be impossible for that child, and which day will be okay. We try to use the "spare" time well, although maybe Ministry wouldn't see it as used efficiently. If 20% of this staff's time is used for other tasks, that's not so bad.

We have block funding but the funding hasn't been raised in four years. We're supposed to somehow raise salaries and still function on the same amount of funding. If you raise salaries 3% a year in the last four years, funding should've been raised $12,000. I know that seems ridiculous, but it's critical. It has got to be there or the system starts deteriorating. We actually over-extended on a promise that we were going to get extra funding a couple of years ago, and we really got ourselves in a fix. We were $11,000 over what we should've been for that year. That ends up coming out of general funds, of course, which affects our regular program.

Yet the same child that we could get nothing for went to another centre and got eight hours a day of funding. That's inequity. I understand that the view is that this centre has some expertise already and doesn't need to develop it, but at the same time, we can't let it slip because what it ends up doing is really slipping. I said the next year, "Ok, we're not taking one more child, because we have to make up some of the money that we've lost," and we actually made it up. We haven't lost anymore.

Then there's always the issue of balancing the number of kids with disabilities in the program. I always have kids on the waiting list, and I have had to say, "We can't always," because it skews the balance badly.

There's also always the challenge of breaking barriers created by people's misconceptions. When somebody comes in with cerebral palsy, they'll say, "Oh, but he can't participate in the activity and so, why would he be there?" It used to be that way with Down Syndrome. The bar has been raised, but we need to always be raising it because every time something else comes up, you'll have a bar.

What is your wish list for the centre?

Money. Besides money? Staffing is an issue. We don't have enough qualified staff.

Right now, we are working with a new person who could potentially become a staff member, but I'm not sure how good she's going to be. I walk in and she's sitting at the table. I've seldom seen her off her butt. She's sincere. She's nice. She wouldn't hurt a kid. But it takes a little more than that, you know. She was doing just a half an hour a day with one of the kids with special needs, and I had to plan it out for her every day because her idea of being with him was to sit beside his wheelchair.

Talk to me about your vision for inclusion.

It would be that the kids could be included in any centre and would find all centres programmed appropriately. The resources would be there – not only the resources in terms of paying somebody, but the human resources and skills. You can't just pay somebody to sit there. The person has to have an understanding of what the child is about and what inclusion is about. When inclusion first started happening, there were things available to support people to take on children with special needs. That's fallen off a bit. There's this false idea that, "OK, we're all doing inclusion now." It isn't really there. It really isn't.

I know of a major child care centre that has yet to have a child with special needs. Now, this may change since their director of many years just retired. Another nearby centre has had a few, but if they become behaviour problems, they dismiss them or refer them to us. It happens fairly regularly. So I wish for child care centres to have some kind of an understanding that you make it work and you don't just cop out because some parent has complained because a child with needs has hit his kid, or something like that has occurred.

I just don't consider asking a child to leave or referring a child elsewhere as an option. We work out the problem and provide the supports to make it okay. I don't think that people are encouraged to do that enough. In most cases, if your Board of Directors says you have to get rid of a child, then the family is given notice. I think there needs to be a rethinking of how that works.

We've only had to ask one child to leave in 27 years. That child was deeply disturbed and probably sociopathic. He's still in school in a small class, but he's on medication now in order to control his behaviour. He just hurt too many kids so we couldn't provide safety for other kids. If we could have had support for that child, we probably would've kept him. He's the only one in 27 years. I still visit him regularly. I've stayed friendly with the family....

8

"We Don't Say 'No' to Any Child"

This is a center that has maintained and even increased its inclusion quality. Returning after twelve years, I found them a little more skilled, a little more committed – rooted even more deeply in the community and in their own program. Since they were already known for doing an extremely good job, especially with children with autism, their provincial government has been wise enough to provide support and not set up barriers. They've faced changes, such as unionization, expanded enrollment and enlarged facilities. But finally, this centre did not seem tired, and inclusion seemed safe in their hands.

What made the difference? Was it stronger provincial support for inclusion and child care in general? Government provides therapies on an outreach basis right in the centres, and while salaries are still low they have increased. ECEs in this province are cautiously optimistic about their future. Perhaps it's the consistency of having had the same director. Perhaps it's the director's courage to unapologetically use one-to-one techniques in the face of current dogma that says services should always be delivered in the group. Perhaps it's the courage to have identified support staff who did not have formal training, who seem to be "naturals" – and others whose training

was informal and valuable, such as the person who grew up in a home where the parents fostered children with special needs.

Sharon Hope Irwin: How has your centre changed with regards to the inclusion of children with special needs during the past ten years?

Centre Director: What seems to have happened most recently is that we've encountered difficulty hiring staff. That has had the biggest impact on us. It has meant that maybe we haven't been able to enroll children that we might otherwise have been able to enroll had we had quality staff.

I don't even necessarily mean specially trained staff at this point, although clearly there's a crisis in the field with that. I just mean quality staff who are able to pick up the skills it takes and really understand what it means to work with a child with special needs within the program and meet that child's needs together with the centre's needs. We continue to expect that our staff will get to know the child, understand the child, and understand the child's needs and the child's family. They are expected to work as a team with the other staff and share information in a way that is best for the child and the family.

That is something that could be in danger of changing because we aren't always able to get the people that we want. So finding that kind of staff is what we have struggled with most. If we gave less, that really would compromise the program.

I think our goals for including the kids with special needs have remained the same. We strive to meet the children's needs in the most meaningful and comfortable way and the families' needs, as well. In terms of the inclusion part, we have always accepted the fact that children often come in needing more support than they will need when they leave. In fact, one of our goals is to see that growth over the time the child is with us. There will probably be more one-to-one time in the beginning and less in the end when the child is able to participate in more things and understand what's happening.

My next question has to do with the maintenance of inclusion quality in your program were you to retire or to leave for another program. How deep are the roots if you were to go?

I've sunk those roots in so deep they wouldn't even know what's hit them! I've hammered away! We spend quite a bit of time at staff meetings talking about the children with special needs. Where are they? Where are they at? What is the person that's responsible for their program doing? What goals are they currently working on? We make sure that all the staff is aware of what's needed. We've brought in outside people when we've needed to do that. That would continue – I can say with confidence that it would. Everyone's style is a little bit different so there would be new approaches, but I would hope that there would continue to be growth.

An especially important aspect of our program has been the visibility of adults who are wheelchair users, and/or have communication difficulties, who live in our building. Kids and staff see adults with disabilities all the time and feel comfortable saying hello, chatting, walking down the hall with them.

It's also important to remember that we do not do this all alone. Through government, we have Child Development Counsellors, a Behavioural Specialist at the Child

Care Office, an Autism Outreach Program, close contact with the Child Development Clinic and, of course, funding support from Child Day Care and the Children with Special Needs program.

Within our centre, we have a team leader for the Special Needs Program. She is someone who's been here since we enrolled the very first child identified with special needs coming into the centre. So she is well aware of where we are philosophically, how we establish goals, and how we work with families and other staff.

The team leader meets with the staff identified as working with children with special needs. She also meets with the Child Development Counselor who usually comes in bi-weekly. She meets with the speech therapists, occupational therapists, all of the people that support the child with special needs. She will be there at the intake meetings so, having had that initial contact with families, she continues to maintain that throughout.

And over time, many staff have chosen to take on the special needs support role for a particular child, while I hire someone else to be the ECE for a time. So there's lots of knowledge and experience among us.

During our staff meetings, we break into our groups, and each staff goes into their classroom and does their planning. Then, the team leader will take those staff who work with kids with special needs aside and discuss any issues or concerns that they might have. That individual consultation takes place after the team leader has already met with all of us as a group and has had some of that discussion as well. She works a little bit more intensively with the people who require it.

How do you orchestrate the special needs support staff in your child care centre?

What we have tried to do is, as children have come in, we identify the children with lesser need for a one-to-one. That way, when the staff person comes into the group of the child with special needs, the special needs support staff lowers the ratio.

This works well when a child doesn't need as much direct intervention. The support person can work with the child as part of a group, and she can do meetings with resource people. The funding for her comes through the funding that specific child receives, so her amount of time off the floor during the day is minimal. It depends on how often the resource people are coming in. She may be off the floor to meet with a resource person but, even then, she's still directly involved in the program for children with special needs. That's where the funding comes from.

In our centre, the support workers, who are one-to-one workers on contract, work under the special needs team leader who, in theory, has a morning a week to do everything else associated with having children with special needs here. I used to do this all by myself. The team leader also does direct work with children during the day – she is responsible for two children with special needs – one in the morning and one in the afternoon – who require one-to-one attention. And there's always something else. We are not funded for support workers' breaks, lunch periods, their absences, or meetings with therapists. You know, you saw the nutrition assistant preparing snacks while keeping her eye on the child with autism, who was sitting alone at a nearby table, occasionally watching the other children at Circle.

What about your general staff? Do you think that if they had the opportunity not to have these kids in their programs they'd be happier?

Man, that's a nasty question. I don't think that they would be. I mean, I say that loosely. Has it been difficult sometimes? Yes.

Last year, we had very needy children – children who were very affected. So when you have children in the group who cannot be alone for two seconds because, unattended, they're on top of something – they have no language and they're screaming, or they're grabbing something from other children, or a child has built something and they've just bowled over it because they don't understand – that is truly difficult.

Would it be easier without those kids? Definitely. It would be easier. But easier is not necessarily more fulfilling or better. So I don't think the staff would rather not do the program. I don't think they would but, you know, that's a hard question, because maybe they would. Maybe they would talk about how difficult it has sometimes been on the other children. Maybe the staff who watched the child with special needs kicking furiously at other children yesterday before she could get right there, and the fact that some children were crying in the end, maybe she would say it's simply not fair to the other children....

Do you think your Board would take a proactive role in promoting inclusion if you were to leave the program?

Yes. Right from the beginning, there's been our Board. Our long-time Board chairperson worked in this building, which is a residence, with apartments and support services for adults with disabilities and elderly persons. Also, there have been an occupational therapist and a physiotherapist – also from the building – on the Board most of the time. And parents of children with special needs have also been board members on a regular basis.

Board members such as these would "keep us honest," would serve as a counterbalance, if I or my successor lost the commitment to inclusion.

They understand that inclusion has been an integral part of what we have done and that we have seen the value in doing that. We have the satisfaction that we've received when families with children with special needs have left the centre and talked about how much their child has gained and grown and how much they, as a family, have gained and the value that it's brought to them. As a program, we are there to meet the needs of all children. Our Child Care Centre doesn't have in brackets after its name, "Able-Bodied, Cognitively-Abled Children Only Need Apply." That's not who we are. The Board has a solid understanding of that piece – of who we are.

Over the last year or two, we have been working on getting another building finished and that has taken a lot of effort and energy. Once we're there and settled, we'll get back to our focus on the real priorities. But this project has definitely been in the best interest of all in terms of our ability to better meet the needs of children with disabilities on-site.

Some parents, who now have to come to the child care centre, pick up their children, and take them for speech therapy during the day, may be able to hook up with those services right in the new centre, since it's housed in a hospital. They can still come, maybe, and participate, or a staff person can also handle that.

We have had speech therapy students come along with the speech therapist before, but there may be more opportunity here, when we are in our new building, for the students to actually come and spend part of their practicum with us and get involved that way.

Looking back on your program's history, where do you see your centre's biggest successes in maintaining or extending inclusionary child care service?

The way in which we have been open to the professionals who have come in to us has made for successes. We have done the Train the Trainer Model, and I think that has been a part of what we've done right. We've been open to that. "You know it all. You come in, and you share it with us so that we can share it with the children."

Also, we have been keen to access any support that's been available to us and keen to access any information relevant to our program, hoping to better understand what parents are looking for and how they want to see this happen for their child. What sort of vision are they coming in with?

If there's been success for us, it's been through our openness and search for greater knowledge.

Can you think of areas where there are persistent problems in maintaining or promoting inclusion? Frustrators? Barriers?

The school system sometimes presents barriers perhaps. And I need to rephrase that because maybe it hasn't been the system but more a particular teacher in a particular classroom. I say that loosely, and I say that lightly, because that hasn't always been the case. It hasn't been a huge barrier for us, but I can think of one or two occasions over ten years when maybe we've thought, "Hmmmm, is this going to fly in that classroom? The teacher doesn't seem to really be open to what we're saying."

Then, on the other hand, I've had principals who have asked me to come in and speak to all the teachers in the school because our child is going to move from kinder-garten through to Grade Six, and all the teachers should be aware of this child, what the child's needs are, and how are we going to best integrate a program at the school. So I can't say that there have been any consistent barriers. I think we've been very fortunate.

Do you find that parents of typically-developing kids feel concerned about kids with special needs who are aggressive or violent? Is that ever a problem for you?

It was yesterday. Just as a mom was standing there telling us, "Gee, my daughter seems not to want to come to child care these last three days. She talks about a child poking her, pulling her hair, and stepping on her" – the child engaged in that same behaviour. The mom said to the staff, "Oh, that must be him."

It's not a problem directly tied to any child with special needs. It can be a problem with a child with no special needs. Either way, behavioural issues cause parents concern. This hasn't been such a problem for us that parents have come and said, "I'm taking my child out." That has not been the case.

Have you ever had to suggest that a child go elsewhere after the child had been in your centre for a while?

No, not for children with special needs. I've had typical children with whom I've had to say to the parents, "This may not be the best setting...This isn't working out...Your child is aggressive...."

Actually, in the last year, I've had staff who have said, "It's him or me." But, again, that wasn't a child with "special needs." I'm differentiating between a child with special needs and one who has *no* identified special needs, and does not have a support staff, but has aggressive tendencies.

Is there a story that you keep in mind to remind yourself of why you're doing this difficult work?

The story for me – and it's not a story – is simple. This just matters. The children who we've had in the program matter. Children with special needs matter as much as other children. And so, for that reason, what we do is important.

It matters to the parents who often, when they bring their child to us, are still in the process of grieving and they're looking for a place where their child can come and be a child. They've been given a diagnosis. They understand on some level – be it well or poorly – that their child is not like some of the other children in the centre, but they see that their child will be accepted as a child first, and then programmed for later.

I do have two stories for you, one that is very positive about us and another that reflects our growth and development.

You can imagine what our waiting list is like. We have a reputation for, and a commitment to, inclusion, and have been working at it for over twenty years. So lots of parents and consultants come to us. But if we were to enroll every child with a special need, we wouldn't have the inclusive program that everybody wants. [That is, with a mix close to natural proportions of children with special needs.] So, as advocates we try to involve other centres in enrolling these children. I give workshops, consult with other centres and teach a course in Inclusion at the community college.

Well, anyway, this particular mom wasn't working, didn't have a child care space, but was really frazzled by her child with autism. We arranged for her to come in, with him, three mornings a week. She'd support him but would have a child-centred place to do it in, and a chance to see what might interest him. It helped her a lot, I know, and I'd do it again.

On the other side, in a situation that shows our development, let me tell you about a child whom we didn't enroll. I recently met a woman in a grocery store, who told me that she had phoned for a child care space ten or more years ago. When she had told me that her daughter had diabetes, I had been very nervous about including her. I think I may have said, "We'll hold the space for you; we'll get together to figure out what changes we need to make; and then we'll admit your daughter." The woman didn't follow through, and then went elsewhere for her daughter.

Today I'd still say, "Let's figure out what she needs," but diabetes wouldn't be such a challenge.

We're open to whatever comes our way. We don't say "no" to any child.

How do your methods work for people who are involved in Applied Behavoural Analysis (ABA) programs? Is that an issue at the moment?

No, because we have always been really clear on what it is that we do, and providing a specific program like ABA isn't it.

That doesn't mean, though, that we haven't worked together with some people from the ABA program. We have done that. But typically, if parents want that sort of a specific program, eventually the child leaves our program because that's what the parent is looking for. That has happened a couple of times, and that's okay. Parents need to make decisions about what they feel is best for their child.

We're funded by the province. The province sends us people from their Autism Outreach Program, and we follow through with their recommendations. They currently have three people employed with that outreach. They consult with child care centres that have enrolled children with autism. They come to the child care centre and engage in a Train-the-Trainer model once a week for around five weeks. They meet with staff and with parents.

This allows the staff person at the child care centre to take "Autism 101," as they call it, and get a better understanding of what autism is developmentally, physically, cognitively, emotionally, socially, and what kinds of behaviours the child may display, and how we might best work with the child in order to keep it meaningful and comfortable for that child.

This has been huge for us. We have sucked up everything that we possibly could from them, in particular, during the first few years when it was relatively new to us. Together we have come to the point where we have a really solid understanding. The other thing, too, is that the Autism Outreach Program is on the edge in terms of knowing what the latest research is. If there is something out there that someone has found to work really well, they're bringing that to us. And we're looking for that. We want them to bring it to us.

For me, personally, children with autism are just an incredible group of kids, and if, in some way, we have met their needs in the years that they have been with us, then we've done a good thing.

One thing that interests me about your present centre is its location. You're on the ground level, but on the next floor up and on the other floors, a number of the people living in the building are in wheelchairs, and a number of the people have other disabilities. Has the fact that many of the people in the building have visible handicaps or disabilities had any effect on your kids or your staff?

Children have become accustomed to seeing people who have needs, as people first. That example of a child who is out in the shopping centre and sees a person in a wheelchair and points, "Oh my! What's that? What's wrong with him?" doesn't apply here. I think that the children in our child care centre would have a clear understanding of why a person might be in a wheelchair. They wouldn't be awestruck by that. They'd just think, "Oh look, there's someone in a wheelchair. They have a wheelchair because their legs don't work like my legs work, and the wheelchair helps them to get around the stores."

We've had some of the people with disabilities in this building actually come in and talk to the children about what's happened to them, why they're in a wheelchair, how their motorized wheelchair works – things like that. We also had a person with a disability who volunteered in the child care centre for a really long time. Not only was she in a wheelchair, but she didn't have any language either, and the children quickly learned what she meant when she pointed or vocalized or made sounds. So it isn't a shock for the children. In fact, there is an acceptance of that person with a disability who just may look a little different from me.

We had a little boy with spina bifida here. I think he was about four years old at the time. We became very concerned about what was he going to do when he grew up. How was he ever going to live alone? How would he ever be able to reach things? So I spoke to the Executive Director upstairs, asking if there was anyone with spina bifida in the building who might be interested in coming and sharing some information with this child or opening their apartment to this child and having the child come there. There was. And he did.

The child's grandma, who he lived with, she came along as well and had a tour of the apartment and spoke with this person. It just simply gave us all better understanding of how he would, in fact, be able to manage out on his own. It was one of those moments. It was just nice.

Other children in our program with special needs have been able to see – if they were in a wheelchair – the other adults who live here and have wheelchairs.

So, again, there's a comfort level with that.

Do you feel the typically developing kids benefit from interacting with kids with special needs?

I think that there's a definite benefit because it's an opportunity for them to see something different and to understand it, rather than to be fearful, because I think there's a human tendency to fear what is different. There is an early realization for the children at the child care centre that there is nothing to fear here. They learn, "Perhaps, I need to talk a little bit slower, perhaps if I move a little bit slower, then this child can participate." Or, in some cases, "If I move a little bit faster, I can keep up!"

Some children clearly become helpers and, sometimes, through being a helper, there's a friendship that grows. Sometimes, when kids are asked to be helpers, it doesn't necessarily mean friend, and I see that, with some of the children, they're very willing to help, but when it comes to really playing, off they go. That's something we've talked about as a staff. What's the game here? How are the children playing? And how often are you asking a typically-developing child to come and be a helper?

And, if you're doing that, are you doing the reverse, as well, and asking the child with some needs to be a helper to the typical child where the child with special needs has some real strong abilities, because they all do.

Nurturing friendships is a difficult task. I talk about that when I teach the course at the college. What I'm saying to students is just stop and think about that. Just stop and think about it.

Give me your current picture or vision of what you mean by inclusive child care.

You know, I don't think that vision has really changed for us. For us, inclusive child care has meant that we're providing services and programs in environments for all children. For a child that's coming in with some identified special needs, I think that we have a responsibility to understand what those are and what fits for that child. Again, you know, meaningful and comfortable.

If the child is just there and it's not meaningful and it's not comfortable, we're really not meeting the needs of that child. And so, it's a process, and we move from A to B to C, and we move always keeping the child's interests at the forefront.

We had a child – a little one with spina bifida – who came in and was *extremely* fearful of all of the other children. He came from a family setting where the provider had actually kept him away, physically, from others. There was a barrier between him and the other children. He was in a lower wheelchair that made it possible for him to be on the ground, but forget it. There was just no way. He was deathly afraid.

When he started, he spent more time upstairs in an administrative office and little bits of time with the children in the child care centre. For him, the inclusive child care experience began there and, from there, he went on to more and more time with the kids to the point where he could be down on the floor with the kids and engaging in play with absolutely no fear at all.

So, for me, inclusive child care means that we're meeting the needs of the kids. Period. I mean, it doesn't mean that he comes in and stays apart. To me, that's not including him. He physically has to be with us. At first, he spent more time upstairs. Then, it was outside the elevator with a staff and a book and a puzzle, or whatever, but being able to see the kids as they moved. Perhaps walking alongside of them, but not exactly with them.

That child, in particular, is a huge success story because his progress is really clear. I'd never had a child come into the program who couldn't even physically be in the child care centre. We thought it might take a long time for him to get comfortable but it just took a couple of weeks.

We have taken a similar approach with kids with autism. They go through a process of getting closer to the group, of being observers for a little while, of doing a lot of one-to-one things until they – some of them – are ready to participate more fully. The strategy is to move the child into the full program as he's ready. Philosophically that's certainly how we've looked at it. We start a program within a program and then merge it in comfortably. That's how we've often described it to parents when they've asked, "What is this going to look like? My child can't sit for circle time."

I still remember a little girl who would play at the water table, and we could see that she'd be glancing over at story time when the other kids would be sitting down. We thought, "Well, we'll move the water table closer. The damn thing can be picked up! What's wrong with us?!" And so we did that. We moved it over three feet. Then she was two steps away from the other children and four steps away from the story. So, you know, what's wrong with that?

What is your current wish list for the centre. If money weren't an issue, what would you have for your program?

My wish list right now would be to have a strong core of applicants from which to hire. You know, that seems to be a huge problem right now.

I also want nice, bright places for the kids. I walked into the Credit Union on Friday to finalize some of our loans for the new building and the move, and I got offended by how much nicer their facilities were than the ones we have for the kids.

I said to the girl there, as I walked into her office and was blinded by the light – I said to her, "Excuse me, and forgive me, but I'm offended by the amount of windows in this building."

She looked at me like I was crazy. "What are you talking about?"

"Well, you have to understand I'm with a child care centre, and we're building right now and I've had to fight tooth and nail, and I've had to say, 'No' to some windows and some natural light because of finances. And I see that here it's just not an issue."

I had a similar reaction at the car dealership. Those damn cars have more natural light in their building than our kids do in theirs. Cars! They're just sitting there. They're not living, breathing things, and they have more natural light than a number of children who spend all day long in child care centres. So that's my newest thing.

We have lots of natural light in this new space, but we would have had more had there been money. One might say, "Well, you know, that's private business for you. They can do whatever they want..." I don't give a rat's ass! I'm ready to do a Letter to the Editor. It's offensive that they have so much so easily when these kids get nothing. Parking lot attendants get paid more than child care workers or, you know, the same thing. Anyway, that was my aside.

There is a need for training, but we need the emotional caring part, too. Some people just have their hearts open to kids. You know, I have a grandma right now who is raising three children. Two of them are in our program – children with FAS – and the third one with FAS she has brought up from a tiny, tiny baby. He looked like he was about twelve inches long when he was born. Sometimes I see her with other children, as well. She and her sister provide a foster home. And she's patient and calm, kind and understanding. I don't know where they get it.

I think, when you come at it with passion, as well as skill, then you do what's right almost naturally. It's hard work but, sometimes, you just do it and it doesn't feel

9

"I Don't Believe in Sticker Charts"

Unlike most other centres I visited, this one has had less dependence on the charisma and leadership of the director. It is part of a large community agency that also runs an inclusive after school program, a family day care service, a resource support program to other child care centres that include children with special needs, and various theraputic services. The overall child care manager of the agency seems to be the guiding force for inclusion. This is fortunate, because there has been frequent turnover in the director position over the past dozen years and yet the program's inclusion quality has remained strong.

Of course, the director matters. The current director brings the continuity of having worked as staff in the centre for a number of years. And this centre is one that has grown because the director is growing and has become more confident and more committed to inclusion.

On the other hand, there have been recent government cutbacks in funding for Ratio Enhancement Workers; where the centre used to have four, it now has only one. While the centre's commitment is there, government policy is undercutting the future of successful inclusion.

Sharon Hope Irwin: How has your centre changed with regard to the inclusion of children with special needs during the past ten years?

Centre Director: We've moved away from assigning a specific Key Worker to work with a specific child, and we've developed a more inclusive atmosphere with teamwork. We've found it works better to have all staff members fully involved with all of the children in the program.

The term "Key Worker" has been sort of put to shame now. I mean, we do this all the time with children with special needs and handicapped children – try to figure out what the right terminology is – and the Key Worker has definitely become one of those words that is just not accepted so much anymore. The people who used to be called Key Workers, whose jobs were to work one-on-one with the children with disabilities, have now become known as "Ratio Enhancement Staff," who are extra staff working in the room because there is a child in the room with a disability.

Even though there is a Ratio Enhancement Staff in the classroom, all staff are expected to be aware of, and to work with, all children. Our goal is that you will never walk into the classroom and say, "Oh! That child is a child with special needs because that person is obviously working with him separately."

It was not an easy change to make. There are still difficulties with the outside perception of what a Key Worker is supposed to be doing. It's much more work for the staff to not only develop their room's program for all the children, but also to work on adapting the program to include the child who is receiving some extra education or therapy.

One of our biggest challenges comes when a therapist

wants to speak with a child's Key Worker, because then I say that the child doesn't have a Key Worker. Well, all their funding is attached to the idea of a Key Worker. Outside teachers and the therapists are expecting the child to have a Key Worker. We have to explain that we are an inclusive program. We believe that all the children are equal. We don't work with the disability; we work with each child, so our team works together to create an environment that is appropriate for all children.

We alternate weekly so that each teacher in a child's class meets with the child's therapists. Then, at the teachers' planning meetings, or with their own communication books, or with the communication board that they have, they write up a brief of the discussion with the therapist and what we're working on this week. So, it's a lot of extra work for the staff to keep that going because it would be easier just to say, "Your job is Key Worker to this child and that's all you do." That would be very simple.

The therapists have grown more accustomed to how we do things at this centre now, but they still try to separate the kids and have them one-on-one, especially when testing is being done. That's the one and only time I'm okay with them working one-on-one, although I still don't believe it's the best way to do testing.

At any other time, the therapists must take a group of children aside, or they must integrate themselves into the room's program and sit at the table with all children and do what they're doing with the child they've come to work with. They can take a small group out; however, I encourage and prefer that they integrate themselves into the room. If they come when the kids are outside, that's too bad; they have to integrate into what's going on outside. We're lucky in the way the therapists do work with us. We are at an advantage because the therapists know from the outset that we are an inclusive program. (In this case, the therapists tend to be more accepting of this centre's approach because they are actually hired by the umbrella agency.)

Tell me more about how this Ratio Enhancement model works.

Our Ratio Enhancement Staff aren't funded directly. Their funding is attached to particular children. We take the three staff in the room, add all their wages up together and divide that by the number of staff in the room, and that becomes the wage that is paid. Government assigns the funding to one person, knowing that all three people in the room are involved.

When a child with special needs leaves, we get two weeks' notice. If one of my children who had funding left the program tomorrow, I would have two weeks' notice and then I would no longer receive funding for the Ratio Enhancement Staff. I haven't had to deal with that yet. The children that we've had have always stayed for the whole year. So far, I've never had one leave halfway through. I have just known that at the end of July these children are leaving, so I'd staff my summer accordingly, knowing that these children will be gone. If it was to happen tomorrow and I lost a child, I would probably have to let somebody go.

In July and August, staff usually go on vacations, so I need staff to cover vacations. The summer vacation staff usually just stay on in September when we get new kids. Generally, we have a child who is funded in each classroom.

Last year, I had four Ratio Enhancement Staff, and this year I have only one. There's not as much funding for children with disabilities. Their budget was filled, so that means that some of our classrooms now have two staff instead of three. That was a big shocker. In the summer, we had four staff in a room and now only two. That's hard to deal with, but the staff gets into the routine of things because they still have fifteen or sixteen children to take care of. There's not much time to wallow around. You sort of just kind of suck things in and get on with it, which the staff does, and they do it well.

One of my biggest successes was in getting the child care accreditation program to recognize that Ratio Enhancement Staff deliver quality direct child care.

When the government first came out with the accreditation dollars and the wage enhancements, Key Workers, as they called them, did not qualify for that funding. I met with my licensing officer and questioned her about why, in a program where we have an inclusive philosophy and staff who all work in direct child care with all the children, they would not then receive that funding. She called her supervisor in front of me and asked the question. On the spot, it was decided. They said, "You know what? You're right. You can apply for accreditation money for your Ratio Enhancement Staff." I said, "Oh great! Can you put that in writing?" She put it in writing, and it was a done deal.

I was very happy I had pushed that because they really just figured that, if you're a Key Worker you work with one child, and you're not actually in child care, so you don't receive the money. I didn't think of it that way.

I don't know then whether they followed up and allowed other centres the same funding. I've actually always sat here quietly thinking, "I wonder if one day they're going to realize what they've done and come back?" That is why I wanted it in writing. I believe they did actually issue a letter stating that Ratio Enhancement Staff would qualify. Centres funded the way we are have all made the change from Key Worker to Ratio Enhancement.

I have never hired a Ratio Enhancement Staff, and I think that is an important point. When I need staff in the child care centre, I advertise for Child Care Staff, and when I hire somebody, even though I know that I need a Ratio Enhancement Staff because I have a child with a disability coming in, I am hiring a staff member.

Nobody here is ever employed with the understanding that they are going to have a Key Worker type job. They're hired as part of a child care team to deliver the program to all children in the centre. Of course, I am interested in their experiences with kids with special needs. Even if I had no children with special needs, our inclusive program is still very pertinent and key, so I do have a lot of questions regarding inclusive practice in my interview for any staff. I even asked the Cook/Housekeeper about her views on inclusion.

When we interview people, not only do we have a verbal interview, we also have a working interview. Lots of people can talk really well but can't translate that into practice, so we have the working interview.

I would really hope that, when somebody has an interview with me, they get a sense of what our beliefs are here. Then they have a decision to make too. "Are we the right centre for them?" As well, we ask, "Are they the right staff for us?" It definitely has to be a two-way agreement. I had one staff who worked here for a couple of weeks and, finally, she just said this wasn't the place for her. She had too much difficulty with the children's behaviours. Her own personal values were that children should not swear or be rude. Her personal values ran a little bit too deep for her to be open to working with these children.

It has been a challenge to keep our enhanced ratios constant, particularly in the last little while. We have noticed that we may have four children with diagnoses in the centre, but we have fifteen children that we believe could get diagnosed. Last summer was quite a challenge. We had several very high needs children who were not diagnosed with anything but may well have been able to be diagnosed. Parent refusals, family situations – there are a whole gamut of reasons why children don't get assessed.

These were just some difficult children. Children come in all shapes and sizes, you know, and some of them are a little more challenging than others, so last year we did have quite a challenging group. It creates a strain when you have a ratio in place for staff to help maintain a program for a child with a disability and those staff become very involved with all the children that have challenges.

Having Ratio Enhancement Staff does sometimes take away from the children with identified needs. We know the specific child in the class that has a program set up and yet there's another child who is really having difficulties and challenges. We are divided among the children so sometimes that Ratio Enhancement Staff may spend a little bit more time with another child that has a difficulty.

As I mentioned, we had a very trying time last year with quite a high number of high needs children. This one little five-year-old boy was having some major difficulties with pooping his pants. We had Social Services involved and lots and lots going on for the child yet we didn't have an extra staff for him, per se. Because of the way our program works where we all work together, the staff really just had to pull together and be that much more consistent with helping each other, switching off when things got difficult and being able to give each other time to take turns in order to keep the sanity.

We're not perfect. We still have our ups and downs, and there are still the times that you get into the lulls and you kind of get a little disheartened. That's the time when we regroup and talk about things and sort of re-strategize before we go on to the next challenge. I think it's really important to keep in touch with the staff and how they're feeling, because it's very easy to get run down or low and get into that negative state. This time of year, it's dark when you get up in the morning, and it's dark when you go home. There are never enough hours in the day and it's cold. Keeping the team's spirits up is key.

Why are you seeing fewer children with special needs this year?

Currently, the number of children with disabilities in the program is lower than it has been in the past. This is partly because they've gone to other places and partly because the government has tightened the reins on funding. I imagine that there are more children with diagnosis and disabilities out there. I am assuming that's because it's easier than ever before to get a diagnosis.

A few years ago, one of the directors here knew a doctor – I'm not sure if he was a friend of hers or not – and he would come to the child care centre and perform this sort of service for us. We found that he was a bit of a diagnosis pusher, or whatever you would call it, and we cut ties with him. It was to the point where you could almost say to him, "Do you think this child has Attention Deficit?" and he would say, "Yeah, okay." I mean, it was getting pretty silly. Labeling is bad, but sometimes it's the only way to get services, and I think he thought he was doing a favour.

I'm not a believer in diagnosing children. The only time it's helpful is to get funding and, of course, you can't get funding without a diagnosis.

Once we get the diagnosis, to me it's a moot point. I mean, I don't even always tell the staff the details of the diagnosis if they get the child. I don't make it a priority to say, "We're getting a child who has such-and-such and such-and-such." It's irrelevant unless the child has a specific medical need or we have to use specific protocols to meet their needs. Then, obviously, that's shared with staff.

So a child has autism, what does that mean? Well, it doesn't mean anything to me. I mean, autism can run the gamut. The differences between Child A with autism and Child B with autism can be absolutely phenomenal. And the spectrum of autism is so vast that to be told that a child has autism is not helpful in the day-to-day working of the child. What I want to know is, "What does this child like to do? What does he like to play? What's comforting for the child? What's scary for the child? Does he like to paint, to colour?" You know, those things. Personally, I find autism is a somewhat meaningless word when you're taking care of a child. It's not specific to anything.

Do you think inclusion will survive as part of your program?

I was still in school when I first came here. I actually did a field placement here and got offered a job from my field placement. I started working at the after-school centre when I finished my ECE training.

Inclusive practice was not a big thing when I first started. The Director was a nurse and the Assistant Director was a rehabilitation practitioner. They were not into inclusion. Shortly after I started, they got a new director, who worked with the Child Care Manager to really get things turned around. From then on, I got a lot of my learning about inclusion at work.

I've been here for eight years. I've been the Director since May or June. Years ago, I was a Key Worker and worked specifically with a child with special needs. My shift was scheduled around the shift of that child. Over time, that's changed. I moved over to the preschool child care centre and have been doing child care for the last five years. I was recently offered the position of the Director, and here I remain.

We have been fortunate in having our Child Care Manager, and I sort of hold her responsible for maintaining the integrity of our beliefs, our work with children with disabilities and our inclusive practices. She has been steadfast and stayed very true to what she believes and how she thinks the child care centre should be run. Through the changes in directors, she has been a constant.

I believe that's why there hasn't been much of a transition. In fact, I think things are still improving and we're even more involved just now because our Child Care Manager was not as big a part of the child care program for the last couple of years and then she came back as Child Care Manager.

The child care centre has been our Child Care Manager's life's work, so to speak. She has been involved in it for the last ten years. It's always been a very soft spot in her heart, so she really has been the one true thing through any changes we've had.

The Child Care Manager oversees the running of the program. She's there if I have questions, or if I have challenges or difficulties. She's like a sounding board for me. She's my supervisor, yet she doesn't specifically supervise my day-to-day decisions. My job is to run the child care centre, and that's the expectation, but she is there to question, to give advice.

I question what would happen to inclusion if she left, but I think she has passed enough on to me. I would hope that I had enough behind me to be able to keep things the way they have been. I've learned a tremendous amount from her. I would hope that my vision could guide us if she left and that I would be able to continue on and pass the torch.

Inclusive programs are not going to work if everybody doesn't buy into them. So inclusion was definitely something that I had to develop my own thoughts on and really weigh up what I believe is important for children and what is not. Anybody can sit you down and tell you this is why you should be inclusive, but if that's not where you're coming from there are a billion arguments about why you shouldn't be inclusive.

My own knowledge of inclusive practice, my own belief in it, and my becoming stronger at expressing my views and expressing why I believe it's right, have helped me to persevere. I'm getting more confident.

A few years ago, I wouldn't have been able to say to a therapist, "You know what? I believe that you should use inclusive practice. You can take that child and go do some therapy but, hey, take some more children with you, too." I don't think I would've been able to say that in the past. I would not have been able to back up my own thoughts and beliefs back then. I can now.

What role does your Board play in maintaining or promoting inclusion?

Our Board does not play a large part in maintaining or promoting inclusion. The only staff person who reports directly to the Board is the Executive Director. Board members make centre visits on the premise that they are ensuring that things are in good order, that we're not putting the society at a risk and that we are protecting our assets. They come in a capacity of just checking out the assets that the society holds and that's it.

When you think of your successes with this program, what have been some of the hurdles or barriers that you have managed to deal with?

Working with some of the parents has sometimes been a challenge.

This past year when we had this really difficult child, and his parents kept insisting, "Everything's fine. Everything's fine. Everything's fine." And, you know, it was just as much a struggle all year with the parents as it was with the child. We couldn't get on the same page as the parents.

Funnily enough, now that he's gone into the school system where the school *will* say, "We won't take the child," the parents have come around and he's getting more testing and more involvement with counseling and stuff like that. That came because they had no choice but to admit and address his problems, if they wanted him to go to school.

Parents of typically developing children have their issues, too. We're all very selfish when it comes to our children. I'm the same way. Everybody wants their child to be safe and not to get hurt. It's very difficult for parents to sometimes come at the end of the day and hear that their child was hurt. There are the parents that start to clue into that, "Oh, it's always Johnny that hurts my baby," and there definitely have been many discussions with parents explaining why that child is in the program.

I've been asked many times why we don't kick children out. At a lot of child care centres, if you swear too much, you're gone. That's very common. I have had many children come to the centre after being kicked out of three or four other centres. We're sort of like their last hope. When some of these kids arrived here, I couldn't understand why they were kicked out anyway. Some places are very, very strict because they're pressured by the parents.

We have monthly parent meetings, and we discuss issues that come up. I'm very open with people when they come here. I explain that this is group child care. We consider ourselves to offer quality child care, we strive to be quality child care providers, but I can't promise you that your child will never get hurt. I will do everything that I can to ensure your child's safety, but children are children, and toddlers bite – it's a developmental stage that they're in. So I try to be as open and as fair with people as possible. I'm not just going to sit here and say your child is never going to get a scratch.

Still, there are those parents that question, "How come Johnny hasn't been kicked out? I'm going to leave the program if you don't kick Johnny out." While they have done that in the past, it has not happened while I've been the Program Director. I would say that it was unfortunate that they felt that way, but I still would not kick the child out.

My own daughter was in the daycare centre last year, and she was scratched. I had always known that that time would come. My husband and I had engaged in a lot of discussion because my husband was of the attitude that, "The minute she gets hurt, I'm pulling her out of there and she's never going to daycare." I kept saying to him, "It's group care, and group care has a lot of benefits," but we know there are some negative parts too. She is exposed to other children, illness, and things like that.

Anyway, I went to see her one day, and she just looked completely mauled like somebody had just grabbed her face and scrunched it up and scratched it. As somebody who's worked in direct child care since 1988 and sees just about everything, I was just so mortified that I had to leave and go outside and have a cry. I just was so devastated. To this day, she actually still has a scar on her cheek. So I'm constantly reminded of that, and it wasn't a pleasant experience.

My husband just flipped a lid. He did a lot of, "I'm going to go in and talk to his parents, and I'm going to do this, and I'm going to do that." I did a lot of, "Calm down. Don't be silly. You're overreacting." She turned out to be fine. I, in turn, took that experience and tried to raise my daughter to set boundaries. I tried to empower her to say "No!" and we constantly talk about how you're able to say, "Stop, I don't like that." She's two, but she can tell you, "Stop." This is to teach her that there are other ways that we can deal with things, and that's hopefully what we do with the other children in the centre.

So I understand where the concerned parents who want aggressive kids excluded from the program are coming from. I try to communicate to them why that is not desirable. At our best, we do prepare these kids for that playground world of school where there is less control and less supervision. We hope they'll have some of those playground skills having been in a group setting.

My favourite words in the centre are when I hear a child saying, "I don't like it when you...." It's like music to my ears. We're telling them and teaching them and guiding them into what is acceptable and appropriate. It is appropriate for you to say, "Stop. I don't like that." It's not appropriate for you to go and shove someone against the wall. But let's not focus on the things we don't want them to do – let's focus on what we do want them to do!

Do you have a particular story that, for you, illustrates how your program works?

I'm very proud of this story, and I actually tell it to people all the time when they have problems with swearing.

I think that sometimes you get into a rut where you just can't seem to figure something out. We had a little girl here, and she would swear, swear, swear – and we had really gone through everything, trying different things. Then finally, in working together and talking together, we just came up with what we were going to do. The plan was that we would ignore the swearing and give positive reinforcement to anybody or anything that was close by that wasn't swearing. I mean, whenever a child was standing there just quietly talking, "Wow, Tommy! I love the words you're using! Such happy words" or whatever, and ignoring the swearing completely.

So when this little girl stopped swearing for five seconds, we would say, "Wow! I love the words you're using! You're using nice, happy words!" Within a week, we saw a dramatic difference. By two weeks, for sure, the swearing was absolutely gone. I mean, the game was up. It just took every staff doing exactly the same thing for this child to know, "I'm not going to get any attention from swearing. All my attention is going to come from not swearing." She caught on.

I really believe that it was the consistency of the staff and really – because always it'll get worse before it gets better – sticking to it through that and not falling into, "This isn't working. We've got to change it." They really stayed strong and true to it, and we had great success with that. I'm very proud of that story because, ever since then we really haven't had a swearing problem because they jump right into the method that we used and manage to keep the bad language really under wraps.

It just came down to the basics of what we know about children – positive reinforcement works. You don't need to "time-out" children. You don't need to punish children. All children want is positive reinforcement. They need to know that they count, and that they're important. When she was swearing, nobody chastised her for it. Nobody told her that she was bad, that she was naughty. They just ignored it and sent her the message when she wasn't swearing that, "Hey, you're doing great. You're fabulous. I like your words." I mean, it just filled her up.

I'll tell you another story so you can see why I'm so proud of our methods.

Years ago, there was this little boy here, and as part of my program I would take him to this psychiatric centre for a behaviour modification class of sorts. As his Key Worker back then, long before we had made the changes I've told you about, I would go with him and stay with him and then bring him back. I would sit behind a one-way mirror with the other parents, and watch.

It absolutely appalled me. The children were set up to fail. They were sat down at the table for a snack and it was handed to them very slowly. They had to sit with their hands on their knees and their faces forward. It was very sort of militarized, and they had to do everything a certain way. If they didn't do it the right way, then that was it, they were done. They were sent away from the table and sat in the corner. They were told, "You are not going to get a snack. You are not going to participate."

They threatened these children. The children were manipulated. They had no self-esteem. It was a shocking way to treat children. Shocking. You know, the teacher was really nice. She was a great lady but her philosophy was so different from mine and back then I was still pretty new. I was still on a big learning curve myself. The whole inclusive thing to me was still sort of new so I was still a bit green. Today, I wouldn't be silent about that treatment, not even for a minute!

Our philosophy does not support behaviour modification programs at all. It's not something that we participate in or believe in. I don't believe in sticker charts. I don't believe in Smarties in a jar....

I recognize that many programs do rely on behaviour modification, and I guess it has its time and its place. But for child care, I don't believe that's the right thing. If you're going to be inclusive – but only Johnny has a sticker chart every time he doesn't do something – then how is that inclusive?

What is your wish list for the centre? Dream a bit. What are the key things you want to do to improve the quality of inclusion for kids with disabilities and for all kids?

It would all come down to having more staff. I can't imagine that anything else would matter as much as having highly skilled staff that are motivated. You can have all the toys in the world. You can have the greatest facility in the world, but unless you have the staff who are going to maintain your program so that it works for the children and who understand that children are equal and that children need to be taken care of, not mail-slotted into categories, you cannot ensure a quality program. So I wish I had the money for staffing. I wish that the field was more respected. I wish the ratios were different. I would love to have more staff per child.

I also wish for more family involvement. I would love to see more parent volunteers. Those really are the key important things for me. I'm not really so interested in physical space and things because I just don't believe that that's what ultimately makes a quality program. Toys and space might help, but unless you have the staff and the support of families you can't be a success.

My personal goal right now is to have happy staff who are satisfied. I can't value my staff enough. I join the staff for planning. We've been doing a lot to really get into the specifics of what the kids are interested in. Once we talked and realized that they're not interested in cars and trucks so much as they're interested in horns or things that go "Beep!" Really fine tuning.

That in itself has given a new excitement to the staff because it's different. They're getting away from the general math flow-charting on winter temperatures and stuff like that and getting more into snow. Ice. The cold. This kind of creative brainstorming reveals something that was always there but over time had sort of just slipped down a little bit. Now we're on the uphill slant again and just fine-tuning....

10

"Everywhere You Turn, There is a Question Mark"

Established in 1979, this centre, located in a suburban school building, has included children with special needs since its beginning. The original directors made their mark locally, provincially and nationally when they began to include children with special health care needs, and to do research, resourcing and advocacy on that topic. Since our first visit in 1992, they have expanded to a second location and have fought (with very strong parental support) to stay in their original school setting. Now, as they both move towards retirement, they are trying to set the stage for their successors.

When we visited this centre recently, we realized that while the quality of inclusion was still high, young staff were unaware of the vital history of this centre. They did not know that they were pioneers in including children with special health needs – an example for all of Canada. And I wondered, How will they pass the torch along as the old guard retires? How will they defend inclusion without their history? Is inclusive child care in Canada as fragile as that?

Sharon Hope Irwin: How has your centre changed with regard to the inclusion of children with special needs during the last ten or twelve years?

Centre Director: As far as the goal of inclusion and the approach to inclusion, nothing has changed. I think the commitment is just as strong now as it was then. The numbers of children and parents involved have remained consistent over the years.

The major areas of change have been with staffing, funding, and facilities. Also, the relationship between the centre and the community and between staff and parents has changed.

As far as staffing goes, there have been a number of changes over the years. We've had four or five maternity leaves, and two of those women did not come back. We probably have a lower turnover rate than the provincial average, and we still have key staff who were here when we did the first go-round with this, but we've also had retirements and some moves. A lot of the new staff coming in have either been practicum students in the centre, or have just graduated or are coming from another centre. As far as finding staff who fit into the centre and really understand where the program's coming from, we haven't had major problems with that, just with the reduction of staff.

OK. Funding. Major changes have occurred in that regard, and it's connected to supported child care and the fragility of that program right now. I feel like we've gone backwards. The wheel spun around and, instead of being ahead by a mile, we've just spun in a circle. There were definitely good times for the program, and a hell of a lot of hard work was put into it. I don't know how much of it is going to survive. I guess the biggest thing for us right now is the lack of security about what's going to happen. Just the question marks. Everywhere you turn, there is a question mark. The government approach, the way things are handled, doesn't put you on any solid ground.

There's obviously a significant change in how the government is running the program. Part of the new program is that there will no longer be special needs child care social workers. All of the funding will go to large agencies to make regional decisions. And then the agencies, in turn, will deal with centres. Does this sound like we're spinning wheels here, or what? So the funding piece, we really don't know what the pieces are going to be. Eligibility has changed. Through supported child care, we were able to do clustering but that's no longer the case. So for any child that now, currently, has a diagnosed condition, there can be direct funding to the centre for additional staff, or however you want to work it.

The people on the Board are very strong advocates. Still, I don't think we're going to fight off any of the impending changes because, if you look across government ministries, it's been devastating in so many different areas and I don't think child care is a priority. In fact, just yesterday – and this is a complete aside – there was an interview on the radio when I was driving. Two government ministries were combined, and over 700 people were laid off from those ministeries in the last two years. Child care is not going to get any special treatment in this whole thing.

In our case, we have a long and positive relationship with the agencies involved and the consultants who've been coming in. They know us. They know the program. So there is some flexibility for the agencies to take funding that they're receiving and make that work in centres. In our case, they've looked at children who are not formally diagnosed but who obviously require extra support. They are clustering the children's needs, and are putting an extra support staff in for five hours a day. But the problem with that is – although it's working for us right now, it's making it possible right now – it's not consistent. I can talk just from our centre's point of view, but if you look regionally programs are really hurting. That means kids are hurting and families are hurting.

As far as facilities go, we've had major changes. The school near this centre has closed. We're walking children to the closest school. We were hoping, going back six or eight months, that a community group was going to be able to lease the school. They put a lot of work into developing a community plan before that. We were going to be able to work with them regarding child care. Ultimately, it didn't work out. There's a new commercial tenant who has leased the whole school. So things have really changed with that, and there have been a lot of associated adjustments as far as staffing and hours.

We have also converted to a non-profit society, so there's been a change in the administrative structure as well as the facility, and with all this going on you really need to stay focused on just the reality, the day-to-day piece, too. So it's been a bit of a challenge.

As far as the community goes, the centre itself, although we've had some major upheavals, the parent support is just amazing. We still wouldn't be in this building if it weren't for the parents. They were quite adamant that they wanted the centre here, first to continue and then to be relocated here. We looked at other facilities, but this was just a good space. So we're here. The parents have been great. In fact, they're organizing a fund raiser right now for the society, and we're hoping to get a van to transport kids.

Do you still have kids with special health care needs?

We have two children right now with cerebral palsy who are in wheelchairs. One is partly mobile. The issues around allergies have certainly increased over the years, and we're seeing a lot more of that, so we have just banned peanuts and that sort of thing to prevent anaphylaxis. You're not rocked back on your heels when you have a child come with that type of allergy. Right now, we have three little emergency kits with Epi-pens for the three children.

People don't look at disabilities in the way they used to. That's a real evolution. I think the parents with children with physical disabilities now can have a very strong assumption that there will be a child care space.

For other parents who come into the centre now, it's obvious from their first glance that children with extra support needs are being included and being supported in the program. Sometimes it comes up for discussion. There are some parents who will suggest that maybe their child should play in a different area. Usually that's a response to behavioural things they observe. They don't want their child to get hurt, which is understandable. But that's really the only issue.

The number of kids with special needs waiting for funding on the government wait list has grown dramatically. That's where the relationship with the agency has been so helpful to us, because we've been able to have children come in who would either not be eligible or would just be wait-listed for funding, and we've been able to have the extra staff support to make that possible.

How do you expect the inclusion quality of your

child care centre to be maintained after you leave? What are your thoughts about the possibility of its continuing when you retire, or move on?

I'm confident that the immediate next generation will keep inclusionary practices because there are staff that have been with us for fifteen years, and those individuals are committed. As far as the actual administration and the goal of the program, it's not going to change. We have been working with the consultants over the years as they're coming in. We have a real personal relationship with the consultants because some of them used to work at the centre, and because our centre has a strong reputation. The roots are deep, at least in the next generation of people, and I can't really imagine that changing.

As a society, we have a board now. When we were helping to organize and develop this Board, we attracted people who would promote the continuation of our inclusion program. I hadn't thought of that specifically at the time, but when you look at the parents who are involved, two of them have children witih special needs.

What do you think are your primary successes, the successes of your centre, in terms of developing and expanding our understanding of inclusion?

I think we stand as an example that it can be done. I know that we made a difference for a lot of families and a lot of children. If you had asked me five or six years ago, I would have definitely included the work; it was an incredible ten years of work.

We had dreams of a new partnerships program for special health care in this province, but it's gone. There's no money for community support, so that whole piece was a bright flame that has now gone out as far as support goes, which is really sad. I just feel a great sense of sadness and regret about that. It'll be a long, long time. There are no resources for that module training. I would hope that there are sparks of what could happen, and what did happen for a short time here. Maybe it will catch on again somewhere else.

Is there a child's story that reminds you that this is really worth it?

Oh, there are a number of them. I think of little Kyra who started it all. When she arrived, two of her cousins were at the centre and the parents just assumed that she would be able to come too, but her tracheotomy was a huge challenge for us. Over a three-month period, we put in what, at that time, we needed to feel confident to have her at the centre. It was just an incredible experience and a very successful experience. She went on to have the trach removed eventually and is now – my goodness – she must be in her late teens. I'm not getting older, but she did! So she was really the first....

We've got a little girl right now who's going into Grade One. At three, she was in another good part-day pre-school program but she couldn't get more hours support there, and her mom needed more time. So she started here as well and, for probably six months, she did both centres. Then the mom wanted more hours at our centre so we were able to do that. She is still non-verbal, although she has learned to sign. The fact that she's coping in kindergarten and Grade One now – and to the very best of her abilities – is amazing. Her mom is very, very involved. She's actually on the Board. The feedback and the sense that you get of being a partner in that is very rewarding. I think that sets you up to go on to the next child. You see the potential rewards for that personal helping and assisting you provided to both the family and the children.

Then there is little James. He's not diagnosed but I would say he probably has autistic tendencies. It was a very, very slow and painful process starting him off at the centre. We never did get funding for him although he certainly required one-on-one for a long time. When I say painful, it was painful for him, too, beginning at the centre, just being around that many new people, and having new adults in his life. All of that was really hard for him. So you see each little step – the first time that he does eye contact with another child or in some small way shares a toy or does a group play, the first time he can sit for a bit in circle time. You just see every step of his development and change, and that's there for you the next time you want to start with a new child.

Could you expand a bit about your vision of inclusion in child care?

What's my vision? A safe place. A place where kids can feel secure and feel cared for. I personally don't see boundaries as long as it is a safe setting for the child, for the staff, and for the families. Good child care does not replace children's families but it's a part of their family. It's a part of their supports. I would like to walk into a centre that feels as ideally home-like as you can make it.

The centre's program should provide children with the cornerstones, the building blocks, to be prepared for what comes next. For that to happen, it is important that staff feel supported. You have to have a strong relationship among staff members, knowing that you have a common goal there. There have to be good relationships within the staff and then good relationships within the larger community so that you're working together for the kids.

I wish we had more money to help with these things.

Is there anything you would have done differently if you could go back fifteen years ago?

Run for Premier? Change the government?

What would I have done differently? I would like to have done more, I guess, but there are always limits. I would like to have had more involvement with the parents.

Do you have a wish list for your centre?

My immediate wish is for a van, but that's just a detail. The need is just growing and growing, so it's hard to do a little wish list for the centre in the context of my big wish list for society.

In the long run, I just hope that we can continue and that the community support for the program remains strong. That's such a big thing. My hope and prayer is that we are able to continue to provide the service and survive.

11

After the Voices

Sharon Hope Irwin

This collection of conversations with directors of child care centres that have pioneered inclusion across Canada contributes to the second generation literature (Guralnick, 1997)[1] that asks "What works best under what conditions?" Here, I want to discuss dominant themes that appear in the ten interviews.

Back in 1992, I visited inclusive child care centres across Canada, centres identified as exceptional by child care officials, advocacy organizations and child care associations in each province. Those interviews were published as part of the book, *Integration of Children with Disabilities into Daycare and Afterschool Care Systems*[2]. In 2002, I re-visited ten centres again to see how they were faring with inclusion. Eight consistent themes emerged during those interviews: 1) Enhancing and Expanding Inclusive Child Care or, conversely, Limiting or Retrenching from Inclusive Child Care; 2) Directors' Changing Conceptions of Inclusion; 3) Benefits of Inclusion; 4) Community Impact; 5) External Challenges; 6) The Challenge of Leadership Changes; 7) The Challenge of Staffing; and 8) The Challenge of Physical Facilities.

1)   Enhancing and Expanding Inclusive Child Care or, conversely, Limiting or Retrenching from Inclusive Child Care

During the 1992 interviews, most of the ten centres were already including a natural proportion (about 10%) of children with a full range of levels and types of disabilities. Thus, in that sense, they couldn't get much better.

However, during our re-visits, most directors told us about ways in which they had enhanced their inclusion quality over the previous decade. These changes included better use of external professionals, such as speech and language pathologists, physiotherapists, occupational therapists. Changes also included enrollment of children with a broader range of disabilities (such as severe eating disorders and complex special health needs). Several directors noted that frontline staff were now more a part of the process – more involved in planning, consultations and meetings with therapists.

Many directors told us how they had increased their overall enrollment in order to include more children with special needs while maintaining natural proportions. One centre had added an inclusive after-school program. Another was able to include more children with special needs from their waiting list when they added two new sites.

On the other hand, one director candidly explained that her child care funding and extra support resources had become so limited that she could no longer be proactively inclusive. That centre no longer seeks referrals of children with special needs nor does it continue to have any policy regarding inclusion. Another director explained that her centre no longer enrolled children with moderate-to-severe special needs, mainly because children with special needs who were identified after enrollment occupied all of the available spaces meant for children with special needs.

2) The Directors' Changing Conceptions of Inclusion in Child Care

Throughout these interviews, this much is clear: these directors of inclusive child care centres spend a great deal of time and energy articulating and refining their visions of what inclusion entails. One centre's board has a formal sub-committee devoted to developing the centre's philosophy of inclusion. The directors often define their conceptions of inclusion by explaining what inclusion is not. They say that inclusion is not found in pull-outs or in one-on-one sessions. Inclusion is not promoted by behaviour modification approaches. Inclusion is not mere physical presence in the centre. Inclusion is not mere tolerance. Fundamentally, to most of them, inclusion happens when all children fully participate in group play and routines, each in his or her own fashion, supported by knowledgeable staff and a well-designed environment. Inclusion is true acceptance and appreciation of difference.

3) Benefits of Inclusion

These directors tell us that the benefits of inclusion are far-reaching, that they go beyond the indisputable benefits to children with special needs. Inclusion enriches the lives of typically developing kids as well as the lives of parents of kids with special needs and parents of typically developing kids. All participants' lives are enhanced by the interaction, as well as by learning rare skills such as sign language or Braille. The anecdotes these child care directors shared indicate that they have seen first-hand how fears of difference and the unknown are allayed, how instincts for helping and sharing are awakened, and how sensitivity, empathy and imagination are fostered in inclusive settings. Parental concerns about physical aggression or about typical kids displaying regressive behaviours can usually be handled through discussion, and most agree that the benefits of attending a diverse and tolerant centre outweigh the risks. The exposure is good preparation for the increasingly diverse world beyond child care.

Comments by directors support the growing research base regarding the positive effects of inclusive child care and educational settings on typically developing children (Giangreco, Edelman, & Dennis, 1999[3]; Irwin, 1992[4]; Irwin, 1993[5]; and Peck, Carlson, & Helmstetter, 1992[6]).

4) Impact on Community

The impact of high quality inclusive child care programs goes far beyond benefits to staff, families, and children in that setting.

Seven of the ten directors explicitly spoke about the inclusion advocacy work that they do outside of their own centres. The activities ranged from promoting changes in government policy to organizing no-cost/low-cost workshops on inclusion topics, teaching courses on inclusion at community colleges and universities, and just being a willing listener to other directors who are having difficulties with inclusion issues. Most of the directors also work collaboratively with therapists to enhance the success of their services, and with special education and kindergarten staff as their children move on into the education system.

As noted above, two of the ten centres have cut back their inclusion commitment; and, not surprisingly, those directors did not speak about their inclusion leadership roles. Only one other centre director did not speak about her broader inclusion role. Her centre is a service within a larger resource support agency in which the child care director's role seems to be less of a leadership one than is found in the "stand alone" centres.

These findings help to substantiate research[7] demonstrating the effects of proactive inclusion leadership by the director on frontline staff attitude, confidence and perceived competence in working with children with special needs.

5)   External Challenges

When asked about external challenges to inclusion in their centres during the ten years since we last visited, the directors spoke most often about cuts in funding and staffing, and about inadequate facilities. Increasing costs of providing quality care, loss of revenue from government and huge waiting lists have meant that, in order to remain inclusive, child care centres have had to be creative, pooling staff and stretching resources.

Most directors indicated that, despite funding setbacks, they had managed, with real effort and some hardship, to have a good measure of continuity or progress. Three directors explained that they "were doing it differently" because of the loss of some support staff (special needs coordinator, special needs staff).

However, as noted above, one director explained that because of funding cuts, her centre no longer seeks referrals of children with special needs nor does it continue to have any policy regarding inclusion. She added:

"Before, we could say, 'If we can do, it we'll do it.' We are not that strong anymore. Sad. Now, often, we can't do it. If we do it, we're providing ammunition for the government to say that theirs is a successful way of doing things, which is not the message we want to send because, realistically, we need more. It would strain our capacity in many ways to provide services to kids with needs, by pulling out of our resources rather than government's."

Another centre includes only children with mild disabilities — disabilities unnoticed at time of enrollment.

In addition to direct funding cuts and inadequate facilities, two other external trends (or challenges) are apparent: (a) increased involvement with itinerant resource consultants and related specialists and (b) a change from government-run inclusion supports to agency-based supports.

(a) Increased involvement with external specialists and itinerant resource consultants

Most directors report increased involvement with external specialists (e.g., speech therapists, occupational therapists, physiotherapists). Some report that more therapists are willing to work within the child care setting; but others report that therapists still prefer clinical settings. In most cases, directors report that there is more collaboration with therapists than previously.

Many directors commented on their own greater confidence in the value of play-based learning and their expectation that external professionals will value their expertise, rather than expecting them simply to carry out instructions.

While greater access to such consultative support is generally viewed by these directors as a valuable asset, some indicated that it can create tensions between centres and specialists. "Pull outs" or one-on-one therapeutic and testing sessions do not foster the play-based group environment that many researchers (Giangreco et al, 1999)[8] and staff at successful inclusive centres view as key to meaningful inclusion. Four directors reflected on potential tensions between the expectations of autism treatment personnel and their own beliefs in the efficacy of child-directed, play-based learning.

One director warned that involvement of external specialists before a child comes into the centre can sometimes lead staff to form negative preconceptions about a child's behaviour and unwarranted concerns about their ability to include that child.

Furthermore, where itinerant resource consultants have replaced — not supplemented — in-house resource teachers and where too few hours of extra staffing support are funded, the benefits of having access to these outside professionals are greatly diminished. Directors who have experienced this change either limit the number and complexity of children they enroll or use their relationships with consultants to obtain special treatment under the new system. Tension between their continuing capacity to provide high quality, full inclusion while still providing quality care for all children is heartbreakingly evident in their conversations. Despite the potential downside to having increased outside specialist involvement, the consensus is that the trend toward having more involvement is a positive one, and that the key to making such involvement beneficial for everyone is good communication and information sharing. All of the directors note that having more people involved in a child's care requires clear and consistent communication among all involved and more time for meeting, planning and coordination – a rare commodity in child care.

(b)   Change from government-run inclusion supports to agency management of external supports

In 1992, all ten of the inclusive child care centres were resourced for children with special needs through social workers or consultants who worked for government. By 2002, three of the ten directors reported that non-profit agencies had been contracted to administer inclusion resources, such as itinerant consultancy, extra staffing, specialized equipment, and case-specific training. One director reported huge concerns regarding the new process, particularly as the agency admittedly does not have nearly sufficient funding to supply extra staffing to the centre. Another director reported a similar concern, but felt that she still had capacity to weather some of the storm. In a third example, the external agency is the "parent agency" of the centre itself, so there seems to be a philosophical connection between the two. However, even in that centre, the director reported diminished extra support staffing and the need to stretch resources to include children with special needs. The agency's mandate may no longer be congruent with the centre's, focusing more on maximizing enrolment of children with special needs than on sustaining quality.

Trend-spotters have noticed that a similar move may already be occurring in two more of the provinces we visited, but the shift is not fully complete as yet. While there may be both positive and negative factors in a shift to an agency model of support for inclusion, so far the change seems negative. It has occurred in a way that has taken direct funding away from the inclusive centres and spread it thinly across the system. [See Irwin, Lero & Brophy (2004) for a fuller discussion of this trend.] Many researchers have noted that privatization of supports (from government to non-profit community-based agencies) creates another level of bureaucracy between the direct services (in this case, the child care centres) and the governments that ultimately determine resources and budgets (Scott, 2003).[9]

6) The Challenge of Leadership Changes

All ten inclusive child care centres have been including children with disabilities since the mid-to-late 1970s or early 1980s, and most – nine – retained the original director into the early 1990s. Since our first interviews in 1992, change-over of directors has occurred in three of the centres, and another one is now in process. With retirements and additional opportunities in the early childhood field – such as early intervention programs; family resource and parenting programs; resource and referral programs; resource consulting programs; licensing and monitoring positions; training positions, etc. – it is likely that the pace of further leadership change will increase. In addition, the role of the director has changed in several centres – where once she was an on-site director, she now often juggles her time among multiple sites, making her role less personal and more indirect.

Our most urgent question was: "Do you think that inclusion will continue in your centre when you leave?"

The directors all acknowledged that maintaining their programs is highly intensive and all-consuming, a task requiring passion as well as skill, firm thinking, willingness to challenge the status quo, and boundless energy and creativity. As one director expressed it, for inclusion to thrive, "Everyone involved has to embrace inclusion" – and these directors make it their life's work to get everyone on board.

Two strategies were pointed out by directors as examples of how they were attempting to assure continued inclusion: (a) Selecting board members with a commitment to inclusion, and (b) Recruiting and retaining directors with a commitment to inclusion.

Inclusion Voices

(a)   Selecting board members with a commitment to inclusion

Seven directors stressed the important role of their board in keeping the inclusion commitment alive. Pro-inclusion directors find that they must be involved in active recruitment of appropriate board members, especially parents of children with special needs and related professionals, to assure that the inclusion commitment continues.

One director said that her board plays a key role in "keeping us honest" and in broadening the inclusion commitment beyond the leadership of the current director. Another director spoke of a "disastrous two years" that occurred when a successor director was recruited from outside by the Board, to bring in a new skill set. Aware of their mistake, that Board then hired its new director internally, opting for someone strongly committed to inclusion whose administrative skills, perhaps, required development. Only three centre directors did not see their Boards as critical to inclusion — one has retrenched regarding inclusion and neither recruits board members with a commitment to inclusion nor educates them about inclusion issues; the second is part of a large child care resource agency where the Board's interest in the centre lies mainly in the protection of its assets; and the third is part of a municipal system in which many traditional board functions are carried out at another administrative level.

The trend toward more complex organizational structures – single-site centres expanding enrolment; centres expanding to several sites; centres becoming programs within larger agencies – may create additional challenges for community-based boards, with a greater emphasis on business-oriented professionals. Meaningful policy involvement of parents of enrolled children with special needs and of related health professionals may be difficult to maintain, as the child care centre focuses on economic, regulatory and legal concerns. Sometimes the "inclusion people" get moved into advisory committees rather than policy-making committees and, frankly, are often happy to focus on the specifics of their own children or the children they work with. However, if the Board does not have strong and powerful voices fighting for the inclusion program, the issue of inclusion is likely to lose its central position.

(b)   Recruiting and retaining directors with a commitment to inclusion

All four of the centres that have replaced directors have hired the new one from "inside." In two cases, "outside" hirings were tried but shortly afterward an insider was promoted into that position. In another case, a long-term insider was promoted directly. In the fourth case, several changes in the director position have occurred with the current director hired from inside; but the position itself does not have the leadership potential of the other centres, since this centre is part of a large agency where inclusion leadership is vested in another position. Finally, in the centre currently in leadership transition, the director has mentored her daughter to take over the position. While business gurus debate the pros and cons of inside/outside hiring of CEOs, it may be that in our society where the general commitment to inclusion is still so fragile and unsupported, extensive inclusion apprenticeship may be the best assurance that the inclusion commitment will continue when leadership changes.

In our 1992 study,[10] strong social entrepreneurship was seen as a prevalent characteristic of the directors. Most of them actively sought sources of funding outside of the regular operational categories, were rooted in their centre communities and connected to them through interlocking board memberships and community involvement with a broad range of services, and had been involved in these centres for at least ten years. Five of them had already built more complex systems than single-site child care centres.

In 2002, while none of the directors spoke directly about what had kept them in their centres for an average of two decades, it was obvious that a combination of idealism and challenge – of building and balancing these complex systems in the face of inadequate resources – were part of the answer. The role of leader, the challenge of making inclusion work, the effects of their efforts on children and their families – these were some of the reasons why they had stayed. Perhaps the lack of equivalent challenges also kept some of them in these centres – very few jobs provided similar scope for leadership and change. However, rapid development of the Early Childhood Development sector may soon provide opportunities at the executive director level as well as at the frontline level – opportunities better resourced and funded – that may tempt such people.

After articulating strategies to help assure continued inclusion in their centres, when asked whether they think inclusion will continue when they leave, the directors provided a wide range of responses:

"Yes, but in a different way. I think they will include fewer children with challenging disabilities."

"It has, during the three times that I took maternity leave."

"We are all committed, but government will determine

how many children with disabilities we can continue to serve."

"We are not proactive about inclusion anymore."

"I worry about my replacement."

"The Board will keep us honest."

"The organizational structure will support inclusion, through the position of Child Care Manager, and the general policies of the agency."

"I hope so, with board and staff currently deeply committed to inclusion."

"In order to keep staff and Board commitment alive and encourage the willingness to go 'above and beyond' what is needed, and in order to convince and move those who hold the government purse strings, these programs need successor directors with effective written and oral advocacy skills."

7) The Challenge of Staffing

Eight directors focused on the issues of staff recruitment and retention. The two who did not raise this issue were working in somewhat specialized situations, with long-time staff – a lopsided demographic which will probably cause difficulties later.

All directors agreed that a cohesive and dedicated staff is invaluable and, when asked about "wish lists," the overwhelming call was for more staff training, continued professional development opportunities, better salaries, less turnover, more planning time and more qualified extra staff in the classroom. Staff issues focused on both "general staffing" and "specialized staffing."

In terms of general staffing, directors reported that recruitment is increasingly difficult, and that the quality of skills and commitment of available staff has decreased. Moreover, even if scarce resources are used to orient and train new staff, the likelihood of their staying in the centre and in the field for a significant period of time is very slight. Salaries and benefits just can't compete with other industries – even call centres and retail outlets pay more – and increasingly there is competition from other Early Childhood services, such as junior kindergarten, early learning centres, family resource programs, and early intervention programs. In many provinces, trained Early Childhood Educators are eligible to be classroom assistants, an occupation that pays more and includes many fewer hours of work.

Invariably, directors and boards attempt to create environments that provide support and recognition of the important work of their staff. One director describes her centre's efforts: "When we don't have money, our Board finds other ways to make everybody feel valued. At Christmas, the regular staff doesn't work for a period of a week or so. We have support staff and relief staff whom the children are familiar with come in so that the teachers get a break and are paid over that time. We also have a Teacher Appreciation Day, and the food and the gifts are unbelievable. The Board coordinates all of that. It is a great place to work! We all have our ups and downs, but there is no one here that can say they don't feel valued by our Board."

As to specialized staffing, one centre's director dreams of having a special needs coordinator again. Another would love to be able to have a speech and language pathologist on staff. Long-time directors of centres with established inclusion programs and strong reputations are sometimes able to negotiate supports that would otherwise no longer be available. An issue they all share is the absence of funding recognition of the indirect and administrative costs of carrying out an inclusive child care program. Indirect tasks such as parent meetings, consultations, IPP meetings, and transition to school discussions require staff dedicated to that task and available during work hours.

Many of these directors have linkages with the general child care movement and are advocates for quality child care. They are regularly engaged in public presentations and in lobbying politicians and government officials for support for child care and for additional supports for children with special needs.

8) The Challenge of Physical Facilities

Unlike schools, hospitals and fast-food outlets, very few child care centres are located in buildings designed for their purpose. These ten centres are no exception, and the directors are rightly concerned about inadequate and aging physical facilities.

One director explained that her centre was in danger of closing because of contemporary safety codes that they can not meet. A second director explained that there wasn't an inch of space and that the gym had been turned into an after-school unit. Another said, just as we were leaving, that they had been given notice to vacate their 20-year premises in four months! Still another centre had outgrown its space and was moving into purpose-designed space within a hospital complex — space with windows that she unfavourably compared to an automobile salesroom!! The cars had more light than the kids! The tenth centre was losing its 30-year space-in-a-school, because the school board decided to rent the entire facility to a commercial firm.

In the other five centres, directors seemed oddly resigned to "found" space – space that often did not include such important characteristics as parent viewing areas, convenient playgrounds, staff rooms, soundproofing and sufficient daylight, contiguity of classrooms to each other, etc., etc. Several centres could only be considered "accessible" by a very generous definition – such as one in a two-story house, in which only the walk-out basement and the first floor had accessible entryways, but bathrooms and inside pathways were too narrow for a wheelchair or walker.

Elements of good centre design[11] are part of the wish lists of these directors who, all too often, must settle for barely adequate, deteriorating physical facilities, often with fragile leases. Most directors with centres located in public school classrooms felt that they had the best physical facilities that child care was likely to get. Wish lists for facilities include wheelchair accessibility, bright, sunlit spaces, observation areas, open space for gross motor play and small rooms for group work. These centres want to be able to provide well-constructed playgrounds with safe rubber matting below climbing structures and wheelchair accessibility to all areas.

•

These *Voices* have given us history, warning and direction. With passion and not a little disappointment, they have given us a picture of the status of inclusion of children with special needs in child care in Canada.

Clearly, we cannot re-create the level of passion that borders on obsession – the commitment that drove that generation of directors and child care workers. Nor can we give everybody a disability in their families to help generate future leaders. We cannot simply replicate the social activism that characterizes these people. Nor can we create the social capital and open-handed governmental supports that were present during that period of growth. But we can promote a social climate that supports inclusion and turns what looked like obsession into standard, accepted policy. We can utilize the lessons, the skills and the warnings of these exceptional people to expand the quality and quantity of inclusive child care opportunities for young children with disabilities in Canada.

[1] Guralnick, M. J. (1997). Second generation research in the field of early intervention. In M. J. Guralnick (Ed.), *The effectiveness of early intervention.* MD: Paul H. Brookes Publishing Company.

[2] Irwin, S. H. (1992*). Integration of children with disabilities into daycare and afterschool care systems.* Ottawa: National Welfare Grants, Government of Canada. (Now available from SpeciaLink: The National Centre for Child Care Inclusion. See Web Site: http://www.specialinkcanada.org.)

[3] Giangreco, M. F., Edelman, S.W., & Dennis, R.E. (1999). Vermont's guidelines for related services: Supporting the education of students with disabilities. *Physical Disabilities: Education and Related Services*, Vol. 18, No.1.

[4] Irwin, S. H. (1992).

[5] Irwin, S.H. (1993). *The Specialink Book: On the road to mainstream child care.* Nova Scotia: Breton Books.

[6] Peck, C.A., Chase Furman, G. & Helmstetter, E. (1993). Integrated early childhood programs: Research on the implementation of change in organizational contexts. In C.A. Peck, S.L. Odom & D.D. Bricker (Eds.), *Integrating young children with disabilities into community programs: Ecological perspectives on research and implementation.* MD: Paul H. Brookes.

[7] Irwin, S.H., Lero, D.S., & Brophy, K. (2004). *Inclusion: The next generation in child care in Canada.* Nova Scotia: Breton Books, pp. 85-100.

[8] Giangreco, M. F., Edelman, S.W., & Dennis, R.E. (1999).

[9] Scott, K. (2003). *Funding Matters: The impact of Canada's new funding regime on nonprofit and voluntary organizations. Summary Report.* ON: Canadian Council on Social Development. Web Site: www.ccsd.ca.

[10] Irwin, S. H. (1992).

[11] Olds, A. R. (2001). *Child care design guide.* NY: McGraw-Hill.

References

Giangreco, M. F., Edelman, S.W., & Dennis, R.E. (1999). Vermont's guidelines for related services: Supporting the education of students with disabilities. *Physical Disabilities: Education and Related Services*, Vol. 18, No.1.

Guralnick, M. J. (1997). Second generation research in the field of early intervention. In M. J. Guralnick (Ed.),*The effectiveness of early intervention*. MD: Paul H. Brookes Publishing Company.

Harms, T., Clifford, R.M. & Cryer, D. (1998). *Early childhood environment rating scale, revised edition (ECERS-R)*. NY: Teachers College Press, Columbia University.

Irwin, S. H. (1992). *Integration of children with disabilities into daycare and afterschool care systems*. Ottawa: National Welfare Grants, Government of Canada. (Now available from SpeciaLink: The National Centre for Child Care Inclusion. See Web Site: http://www.specialinkcanada.org.)

Irwin, S.H. (1993). *The Specialink Book: On the road to mainstream child care*. Nova Scotia: Breton Books.

Irwin, S.H. (2001). *The SpeciaLink Inclusion Practices Profile.* Appendix A in Irwin, S.H., Lero, D.S., & Brophy, K. (2004). *Inclusion: The next generation in child care in Canada*. NS: Breton Books. Download from Web Site: http://www.specialinkcanada.org.

Irwin, S.H. (2001b). *The SpeciaLink Inclusion Principles Scale..* Appendix B in Irwin, S.H., Lero, D.S., & Brophy, K. (2004). *Inclusion: The next generation in child care in Canada*. NS: Breton Books. Download from Web Site: http://www.specialinkcanada.org.

Irwin, S.H., Lero, D.S., & Brophy, K. (2004). *Inclusion: The next generation in child care in Canada*. Nova Scotia: Breton Books.

Olds, A. R. (2001). *Child care design guide*. NY: McGraw-Hill.

Peck, C.A., Chase Furman, G. & Helmstetter, E. (1993). Integrated early childhood programs: Research on the implementation of change in organizational contexts. In C.A. Peck, S.L. Odom & D.D. Bricker (Eds.), *Integrating young children with disabilities into community programs: Ecological perspectives on research and implementation*. MD: Paul H. Brookes.

Scott, K. (2003). *Funding Matters: The impact of Canada's new funding regime on nonprofit and voluntary organizations. Summary Report*. ON: Canadian Council on Social Development. Web Site: www.ccsd.ca.

A Quantitative Analysis
of Inclusion Quality
in the Voices Centres

Donna S. Lero, Ph.D., University of Guelph

In addition to Sharon Hope Irwin's interviews with the ten directors, observers collected information about both global quality and
inclusion quality in the centres that were visited. All three observers had been trained in *ECERS-R,*[1] had been provincial coordinators for the *You Bet I Care! (YBIC!)* study,[2] and were given training
in *The Specialink Child Care Inclusion Practices Profile*[3] and *The
SpeciaLink Child Care Principles Scale*[4].

The *ECERS-R* – the most widely used instrument for assessing
program quality– was employed to obtain a measure of global quality. Since no standardized instrument currently exists for assessing inclusion quality in early childhood programs, three measures
were chosen: 1) Item 37 in the *ECERS-R* that specifically pertains
to provisions for children with disabilities, 2) the *SpeciaLink Child
Care Inclusion Practices Profile*, and 3) the *SpeciaLink Child Care
Inclusion Principles Scale*. The use of all three measures enabled
the observers to tap several dimensions of inclusion quality, a
method used in social science research to ensure construct validity.
As well, all three measures had recently been used in *Inclusion:
The Next Generation (ING)* – a study of inclusive child care programs with different types of inclusion supports.

The purpose of this analysis is three-fold:

• First, it presents quantitative information about program
quality and inclusion quality in the *Voices* centres, obtained in 2002;

• Second, it provides an opportunity to compare the *Voices* centres to a large Canadian sample of child care programs obtained in
the *You Bet I Care!* study in 1998 and to data from another sample
of inclusive programs obtained in the Spring of 2001;

• Third, quantitative information about the 10 *Voices* centres
can be examined to determine how scores on the objective measures of global quality and inclusion quality relate to the informa-

tion provided by the centre directors about their programs and the changes that have taken place since 1992, when the centres were identified as ones providing exemplary inclusive care.

Overall Program Quality

The ten centres in the *Voices* sample have global quality scores on the full *ECERS-R* scale that range from a low of 4.60 to a high of 5.91.* The mean was 4.90 – a tenth of a point below a score of 5, the threshold that is considered to distinguish programs that are of good quality that enhance children's development from centres that provide mediocre or inferior quality programs. The scores obtained for this sample can be compared to those obtained in two other Canadian studies. The *You Bet I Care!* sample centres (which included centres that did and did not include children with special needs) had a mean *ECERS-R* score of 4.7, while the 32 inclusive centres that participated in *Inclusion: The Next Generation (ING)* had an average *ECERS-R* score of 4.8.

While average quality scores among the *Voices, YBIC!* and *ING* samples are not appreciably different, it is worth noting that the *Voices* centres tend to cluster more closely around the average, and that no centre in this sample had an *ECERS-R* quality score below 4.25. Table 1 and Figure 1 provide comparative information on global quality scores obtained across the three studies.

Readers should note that the three studies referred to in this analysis were selected for different purposes. The *YBIC!* sample was selected in ways that approximated obtaining a representative sample of child care centres in selected geographic areas within

Table 1

Comparison of Average *ECERS-R* Quality Scores in *Voices, YBIC!* and *ING* Studies

	VOICES (n = 10)	*YBIC!* (n = 223)	*ING* (n = 32)
Average score	4.9	4.7	4.8
Standard deviation	0.5	1.1	1.2
Range of scores	4.25 - 5.90	1.66 - 6.90	2.72 - 6.93

ECERS-R scores can range from 1.0 to 7.0.

seven jurisdictions in Canada. Approximately 70 percent of the 234 participating centres included children with disabilities or special needs (usually only one or two children were included, if any); however only 76 (34%) of the preschool rooms that were observed for the purpose of obtaining *ECERS-R* scores included a child with special needs. The sample centres selected for the study *Inclusion: The Next Generation* all included children with identified special needs and were selected for the purpose of comparing different models of support for inclusion in four provinces.

The *Voices* sample was specifically chosen for the purpose of studying centres that were identified as having provided exemplary inclusive child care in 1992. The *Voices* sites were selected by a triangulation method that involved a disability organization, a government official responsible for child care, and a child care organization in each province — all of whom were asked to identify one or more child care centres that they thought excelled in the inclusion of children with special needs. Centres that appeared on all three lists were selected for this study, and if more than one centre ap-

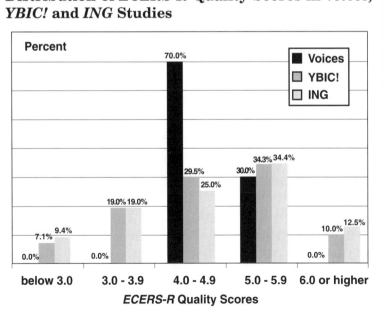

Figure 1

Distribution of *ECERS-R* Quality Scores in *Voices*, *YBIC!* and *ING* Studies

peared on all of them, special consideration was given to centres that displayed unique characteristics related to geography, demographics, or extending the range of children served. Under these circumstances, it would have been surprising if any centre had made that list while exhibiting less than good overall global quality![6]

What these results suggest is that in 2002, the *Voices* centres, on average, approximated the level of overall quality in other studies of Canadian child care programs, including those that include children with special needs. However, none of the *Voices* centres (originally selected as providing exemplary inclusive practice ten years earlier) have scores indicative of low or poor quality – or exceptionally high overall quality – unlike other samples of centres. It is not known whether *Voices* centres' recent scores are higher or lower than in 1992 when they were identified as providing exemplary inclusive practice; however many centres across Canada experienced cutbacks in funding during that period, and the interviews with centre directors attest to some of the challenges they have experienced over time.

Scores of the ten *Voices* centres on the subscales that comprise the *ECERS-R* quality measure do tell an interesting story. As shown in Table 2, there was variation among subscale scores within the *Voices* centres, as is common in other studies. What is particularly interesting is that the *Voices* centres evidence particular strength in three areas: Space and Furnishings, Interactions, and Provi-

Table 2

Comparison of Average *ECERS-R* Quality Subscale Scores in *Voices, YBIC!* and *ING* Studies

	Voices (n = 10)	*YBIC!* (n = 223)	*ING* (n = 32)
Space and Furnishings	5.6	4.9	4.8
Personal Care Routines	4.6	4.7	4.5
Language - Reasoning	4.6	5.0	5.2
Activities	3.4	4.0	4.1
Interactions	6.0	5.4	5.3
Program Structure	5.4	5.2	5.2
Parents and Staff	5.9	4.8	5.1

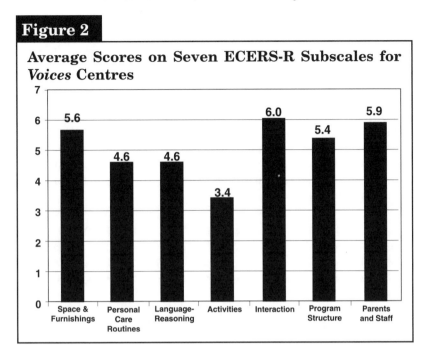

Figure 2

Average Scores on Seven ECERS-R Subscales for *Voices* Centres

sions for Parents and Staff. The 10 *Voices* centres had average scores of 5.5 or above on these three subscales. (See Figure 2.)

The items that relate to space and furnishings include the quality of indoor space, provisions for children's relaxation and comfort, an attractive room arrangement with good traffic flow, and displays of art and other materials for children. Centres that obtain higher scores on these items are likely to be sensitive to children's mobility difficulties and to times when a child (and adult) may need access to quiet space. Such programs are likely to have developed room arrangements that allow children to move freely and easily among activity centres. Displays at children's levels provide more opportunities for learning and may suggest more attention to the kinds of materials that can reinforce concepts.

Items on the subscale that focuses on Interactions relate to the quality of interactions between staff and children, as well as the promotion of positive peer interactions among the children. Programs with sensitive staff who are responsive to the needs of individual children and who promote interactions between children with special needs and their typically developing peers would be expected to have higher scores on this dimension.

Finally, the subscale that relates to parents and staff has items that reflect provisions for involving parents and informing them of their children's experiences, as well as a number of items that relate to provisions to enhance staff's experiences and competencies. Items reflect attention to staff's personal concerns and professional needs, the quality of staff interaction and cooperation, staff continuity, supervision and evaluation of staff, and provision of opportunities for professional growth. Research findings from *Inclusion: the Next Generation* and other studies strongly suggest that these items would be expected to reflect respect for and partnership with parents and a strong focus on supporting staff's efforts and continuing professional development.

Lower scores on subscales dealing with Activities, Language and Reasoning, and Personal Care suggest areas for improvement in these centres that could be remedied by participating in assessment and consultation processes to improve program quality such as those currently underway in several provinces.

The Centres' Standing on Three Measures of Inclusion Quality

Three measures were used to assess the *Voices* centre's level of inclusion quality in 2002. They are Item 37 of the *ECERS-R* scale, which is specific to a centre's and classroom's provisions for children with disabilities, the *Specialink Child Care Inclusion Practices Profile,* and the *Specialink Child Care Inclusion Principles Scale*. Scores on Item 37 of the *ECERS-R* were available for comparison to the *Voices* centres from both the *You Bet I Care!* study and *Inclusion: The Next Generation*. Scores on the two Specialink Child Care Inclusion measures were not utilized in *YBIC!*, but were available for comparative purposes from *Inclusion: The Next Generation*.

ECERS-R Item 37, Provisions for Children with Disabilities

ECERS-R Item #37 includes a variety of indicators of the quality of inclusion practices. Evidence of the indicators is assessed through observations made in a preschool classroom, with follow-up questions posed to the director and/or lead teacher for clarification. Indicators relate to: staff knowledge and the use of assessments for individual children; modifications and adaptations to meet individual needs; the extent of involvement of parents of children with special needs; and the extent to which children with special needs and typically developing children interact in a positive way. As in the other items in this instrument, a score of "1" indicates inadequate provisions, with a score of "3" serving as a threshold between inadequate quality and minimal to mediocre quality provisions. A score of "5" is the threshold between mediocre provisions for inclusion and good quality, and a score of "7" reflects excellent provisions. Item 37 is only scored if the centre/preschool classroom currently has a child with an identified disability in the program.*

The ten centres in the *Voices* sample have scores on this item that range from 3.0 to 7.0 with an average of 5.7. This average is perhaps misleading. Three centres had scores of 3, indicating minimal provisions for children with disabilities. Two centres had a score of 6, indicating a very good level of provisions for children with disabilities; and five centres had scores of 7, indicating excellence in their provisions for children with disabilities.

It is not surprising that none of the *Voices* centres scored below a "3" on this item and that most (seven out of the ten centres) were scored as either a "6" or a "7". The ten centres, it should be remembered, are a purposive sample, identified ten years earlier as especially skillful at including children with disabilities. In the three centres that received a rating of 3, two are the ones that, in the directors' interviews (*Voices*), were described as ones where the directors/centres had retrenched or lessened their level of inclusion. (For the third centre in this group, we have to point to an anomaly in the question — a disconnect between the way the centre works with children with autism and the way that the indicators are phrased.) The two centres that were scored with a rating of 6 are centres that were served through a clinical or pull-out model of professional intervention most of the time.

For comparative purposes, it is known that centres in the *YBIC!* and *ING* samples had slightly lower average scores on this item (5.29 and 5.20, respectively). In both of those studies, scores on this item covered the full range from 1 to 7. None of the *Voices* centres had a score below 3, and none had scores in the middle range either. (See Figure 3.) It is heartening to note that the majority of classrooms in all three studies scored in the upper range on this item (70% of *Voices* centres, 60.5% of *YBIC!* centres,** and 53% of centres in *ING* were scored as a 6 or 7). This suggests that,

---

* While *ECERS-R* scores are usually described as reflecting centre practices, the *ECERS-R* is actually carried out within a preschool room.

** This represents the subset of centres and classrooms that included children with special needs (approximately 1/3 of the larger *YBIC!* sample).

Figure 3

Distribution of *Voices*, *YBIC!* and *ING* Samples on *ECERS-R* Item 37 - Provisions for Children with Disabilities

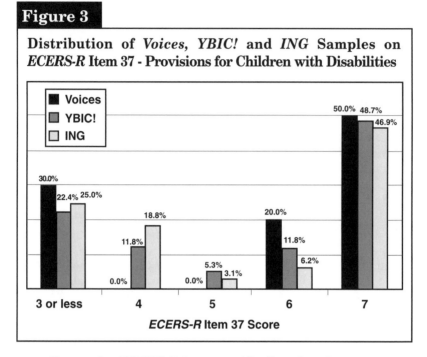

according to the *ECERS-R* item specifically related to provisions for children with disabilities, a majority of classrooms that include children with special needs are observed to make very good or excellent inclusion provisions. Even so, more *Voices* centres (those that were described by their directors as having maintained a strong focus on quality inclusion) had high scores on this item.

The SpeciaLink Child Care Inclusion Practices Profile

The *SpeciaLink Child Care Inclusion Practices Profile*[7] is based on observations in the classroom and centre, and then on questions posed to the centre director, and is designed to assess eleven specific practices related to inclusion. Each item is scored on a scale of 1 to 5, with 1 indicating that only beginning efforts have been made to ensure inclusion quality, while 5 indicates an ideal setting with respect to that specific practice. The eleven items cover practices in the following areas: physical environment, equipment and materials, director's role, support for staff, staff training, therapies, individual program plans, parents of children with special needs, involvement of typically developing children, support from a board of directors or advisory committee, and planning for transition to school.

Overall scores on this 11-item rating scale ranged from 2.90 to 4.91. The mean score was 4.21 (out of a possible 5) with a standard deviation of 0.76. Centres in the *Voices* sample clustered into two groups – three with relatively low scores of 2.90 to 3.30, and seven with high scores on this measure (all above 4.50). The three centres that scored lowest on the *ECERS-R* scored lowest on the *Inclusion Practices* measure, which was not surprising since the two tools tap *some* of the same attributes, and since it seems reasonable to expect that centres that have lessened their level of inclusion would do so on many dimensions of practice. Centres that scored 4.5 or above on the *Inclusion Practices* measure all had ratings of 6 or 7 on item #37 of the *ECERS-R*.

By comparison, the 32 centres in the *ING* sample had scores that ranged from 2.3 to 5.0 and did not display the bimodal distribution evident in the *Voices* centres. The average score among ING centres was 3.7 with a standard deviation of 0.78. In contrast to the *Voices* centres, only 22% of the *ING* centres had a score on this measure of 4.5 or above.

The SpeciaLink Child Care Inclusion Principles Scale

The SpeciaLink Child Care Inclusion Principles Scale[8] is based on five questions posed to the centre director. It was designed to as-

Figure 4

A Comparison of Scores on the SpeciaLink Child Care Inclusion Practices Profile Among Centres in the *Voices* and *ING* Studies

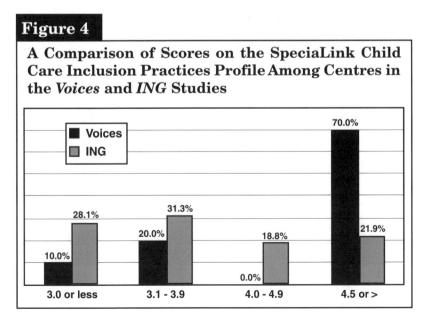

sess the extent to which a centre has adopted principles to guide decisions about enrolling children with special needs and to ensure that their needs are met, as far as possible, within the regular setting. The observers who administered the scale were also asked for their input, particularly if they observed instances where practice appeared to diverge from the principles espoused by the directors. Each item was then scored on a scale of 1 to 5 with a value of 1 indicating that principles are completely undeveloped and a value of 5 indicating that the centre has adopted principles that explicitly support full inclusion and that they are evident in observed practices.

The five items that make up the *SpeciaLink Child Care Inclusion Principles Scale* include: zero reject, naturally occurring proportions, same attendance options (as exist for typically developing children), full participation, and advocacy for inclusion plus maximum feasible parent participation at their level of comfort.

Overall scores on this 5-item scale ranged from 3.0 to 5.0 in the *Voices* centres. The mean was 4.55 with a standard deviation of 0.68.[*] Only one centre had a score on this measure below 4.0, and

---

Figure 5

A Comparison of Scores on the *SpeciaLink Child Care Inclusion Principles Scale* Among Centres in the *Voices* and *ING* Studies

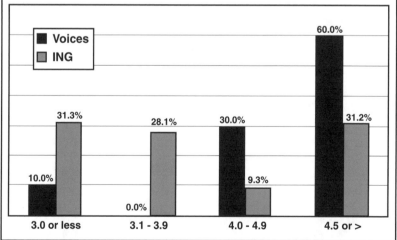

[*] Scores on this measure were not available for one centre.

6 had scores of 4.5 or above, including 5 centres that had a score of 5.0! By comparison, the average score on the *Specialink Child Care Inclusion Principles Scale* among the 32 *ING* centres was 3.61 with a standard deviation of 1.12 and individual scores that ranged from 1.2 to 5.0. Almost a third of the *ING* centres (31.3%) had scores on this measure of 3.0 or lower; and an equivalent number had scores of 4.5 or higher. Once again, with the exception of only a very few centres in the *Voices* sample, most had scores indicating that they had carefully considered and developed standards and principles to insure the full participation of children with disabilities in the program.

The centre that received a rating of 3 is one of the two centres that had lessened its commitment to inclusion; the other centre that had lessened its commitment to inclusion scored a 4.0, a lesser score than seven of the centres, and the same score as the anomalous centre.

A Summary of the Findings on Inclusion Quality

In summarizing the data on inclusion quality in the *Voices* centres we have noted that on each of the three measures: Item 37 of the *ECERS-R*, the *Specialink Child Care Inclusion Practices Profile*, and the *Specialink Child Care Inclusion Principles Scale*, a consistent pattern has emerged. Generally speaking, three of the centres score in the low to moderate end on the measures, while seven centres score very highly, indicating that they have been observed to still be providing a high level of support and to be effective in including children with special needs.

One other comparison was made that confirms this conclusion. Scores on all three measures were considered simultaneously and comparisons were made to the criteria used in *Inclusion: The Next Generation* to distinguish centres that were considered to provide a high level of inclusion quality from those that were not. Centres that met all three of the following criteria were classified as demonstrating high inclusion quality:

- a rating of 7 on *ECERS-R* Item 37,

- a score of 4.3 or higher on the *Specialink Child Care Inclusion Practices Profile,* and

- a score of 4.1 or higher on the *Specialink Child Care Inclusion Principles Scale.*

Inclusion Voices

Using these criteria, five of the ten *Voices* centres would be considered to presently demonstrate a high level of inclusion quality, and two other centres come close to that level, meeting two of the three criteria and having a score that is not far below the cutoff on the third measure. The remaining three centres include two that would fall into the category of evidencing low inclusion quality at this time, and one centre just above that level.

Not surprisingly, the two centres that have scores in the low inclusion quality range are the two where directors described a lessening commitment to inclusion over time. In summary, the quantitative analyses confirm the information provided by the directors in their interviews

In conclusion, the quantitative data presented in this section confirm that in 2002, ten years after having first been identified as centres that were exemplary in inclusion practices, the *Voices* centres, as a group, evidence average levels of overall program quality, but have particular strengths in areas that are likely to reflect sensitivity to the needs of staff, children with special needs, and their parents. On objective measures of inclusion quality, seven of the ten centres still display outstanding levels of inclusion quality. Moreover, centres that do not display high scores on these measures of inclusion quality are described by directors as ones where the focus and commitment to inclusion has lessened over time for various reasons.

These findings confirm the voices of the directors and provide added support that validates the use of these measures in further studies.

[1] Harms, T., Clifford, R.M., & Cryer, D. (1998). *Early childhood environment rating scale, revised edition (ECERS-R)*. NY: Teachers College Press, Columbia University.

[2] Doherty, G., Lero, D.S., Goelman, H., LaGrange, A., & Tougas, J. (2000). *You Bet I Care! A Canada-wide study on wages, working conditions and practices in child care centres*. ON: University of Guelph (Centre for Families, Work and Well-Being). Available from Web Site: http://www.worklifecanada.ca.

[3] Irwin, S.H. (2001a). *The SpeciaLink Inclusion Practices Profile*. In S.H. Irwin, D.S. Lero, & K. Brophy, *Inclusion: The next generation in child care in Canada* (Appendix A). NS: Breton Books. Available from Web Site: http://www.specialinkcanada.org.

Afterword: A Quantitative Analysis

[4] Irwin, S.H. (2001b) *The SpeciaLink Inclusion Principles Scale*. In S.H. Irwin, D.S. Lero, & K. Brophy, *Inclusion: The next generation in child care in Canada* (Appendix B). NS: Breton Books. Available from Web Site: http://www.specialinkcanada.org.

[5] Irwin, S. H., Lero, D.S., & Brophy, K. (2004). *Inclusion: The next generation in child care in Canada*. NS: Breton Books. Available from Web Site: http://www.specialinkcanada.org.

[6] The *YBIC!* authors suspect upward selection bias in their responding centres, because it is likely that centres that were struggling or dissolving were less likely to complete the questionnaires than were centres that were doing well (Doherty et. al., p. 153). The *ING* centres probably show upward selection bias as well, since all were selected by provincial government or agency officials responsible for inclusive child care, who might have a conscious or unconscious desire to have their province appear in a positive light. In addition, US literature on quality in inclusive versus non-inclusive centres (Buysse, V., Wesley, P.W., Bryant, D., & Gardner, D., 1999) suggests a one point quality difference on the *ECERS-R* in favour of the inclusive centres. Anecdotal evidence suggests that centres in Ontario and British Columbia that received either "integrated licenses" or "contracts" to support the attendance of children with special needs as far back as the late 1970s were centres that met implicit or explicit quality criteria of licensing or special needs officials – many of these centres were included in the *ING* sample.

[7] *The SpeciaLink Inclusion Practices Profile* has recently been totally redesigned. A workshop version of the *Profile* is available from SpeciaLink at specialink@ns.sympatico.ca. The 2001 version was, of course, used in this study.

[8] *The SpeciaLink Inclusion Principles Scale* has recently been totally redesigned. A workshop version of the *Principles* is available from SpeciaLink at specialink@ns.sympatico.ca. The 2001 version was, of course, used in this study.

Challenging Books from BRETON BOOKS
The SpeciaLink Series, 2004-2005

For early childhood educators, resource teachers, parents and early interventionists — *anyone* passionate about including children with special needs.

INCLUSION: The Next Generation provides a snapshot of current inclusion practices in child care in Canada. This book investigates what makes inclusion work, what makes quality child care for children with special needs a reality. As we enter the third generation, *Inclusion: The Next Generation* focuses on critical roles and resources that sustain existing inclusive programs and that encourage more centres to enroll children with special needs.

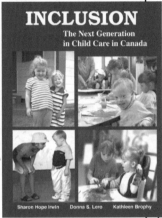

INCLUSION
The Next Generation
in Child Care in Canada

Sharon Hope Irwin   Donna S. Lero   Kathleen Brophy

Price $25.00

Breton Books. ISBN 1-895415-59-4

Charting New Waters — Proceedings of the SpeciaLink National Early Intervention Symposium

Charting New Waters

Contains full text of articles by Dana Brynelson, Debra Martell, Kofi Marfo and Marilyn Peers, plus Alan Mirabelli's assessment of the new shapes of family! Workshops, speeches, face-to-face conversations, & more!
Price $16.00
Breton Books. ISBN 1-895415-13-6

The SpeciaLink Book — On the Road to Mainstream Child Care

SpeciaLink BOOK
On the Road to Mainstream Childcare

This is the story of our road to the principles of full mainstream child care, and of the SpeciaLink Symposium, which made those principles the national agenda for mainstream advocates. Includes reprints of the first 6 SpeciaLink newsletters, a Canadian directory of mainstream child care advocates, a list of further readings, and more.
Price $25.00
Breton Books. ISBN 1-895415-22-5

Inclusion Voices
This book is an inspiring, readable picture of Canada's inclusion journey, told by 10 child care directors. They speak to us directly and without flinching. They provide warnings, guidance and encouragement. A remarkable portrait and a tool we are fortunate to have.

Price $20.00
Breton Books.
ISBN 1-895415-63-2

INCLUSION VOICES
Canadian Child Care Directors Speak Out About Including Children With Special Needs

Sharon Hope Irwin

Integration of Children with Disabilities into Daycare and Afterschool Care Systems

A portrait of 10 Canadian daycares that have developed innovative methods to include children with disabilities. Contains a literature review, an overview of program models, demonstration sites and replication programs, and more. **Price $16.00**

Integration of Children with Disabilities into Daycare and Afterschool Care Systems
Sharon Hope Irwin

Order Form on the Other Side of this Flyer

Prices include shipping and tax.

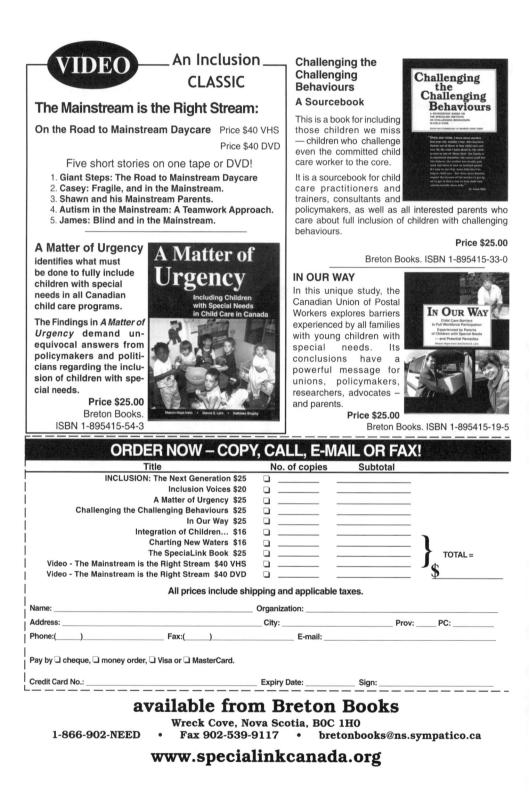